JAPAN OR GERMANY

FREDERIC COLEMAN

JAPAN OR GERMANY

The Inside Story of the Struggle in Siberia

BY

FREDERIC COLEMAN, F.R.G.S.

AUTHOR OF
"OUR BOYS OVER THERE," "FROM MONS TO YPRES WITH
GENERAL FRENCH," "OPEN EYES IN THE ORIENT," ETC.

NEW YORK
GEORGE H. DORAN COMPANY

PRINTED IN THE UNITED STATES OF AMERICA

TO
LOIS

PREFACE

Should Japan go to Siberia? Before a single soldier of the Land of the Rising Sun crosses the frontier of the Russian Far East, and for many years after the Great War has ended, the pros and cons of that question will be debated.

What will the sending of the Japanese army to the Northland mean toward the development of the Far Eastern question and the struggle for the Mastery of the Pacific?

How will Japan emerge from the World War?

What effect will the participation of Japan in the solution of the Russian problem have on the Slav in Siberia and his ultimate destinies?

Some of these queries must needs be left to Time himself for answer. A study of conditions in the Russian Far East and in Japan, extending over the period immediately prefacing the date of the proposal that Japan should send troops to Russian territory, may assist to a better understanding of the situation, at least so far as it can develop until the march of events has carried it beyond its initial stages.

I have been in Japan several times at critical
epochs in her history. I saw Japan and Siberia
in 1916 and again in 1917. In writing this little
book I have no other object in view than to
place before those who are interested something
of what I saw in the Orient and the Far Northeast. I am less of a prophet than a witness.

Should Japan go to Siberia?

By all means Yes, emphatically Yes, if she
goes in the right spirit, and if when she goes a
campaign of education and explanation goes
with her. If Japan is merely to go to guard a
pile of stores from the Huns, or even to prevent Bolsheviki disruption along the path of
the Trans-Siberian, and the echo of the tramp
of her legions bears no other significance than
these, then No, a thousand times No.

If Japan goes with her eyes on the farther
West, and with her goes a group of educators;
sympathetic, understanding, earnest men with
hearts in their breasts and hands of fellowship
outstretched to the Russian in Siberia, who
knows what may not come from such co-operation?

May the day not dawn when the Russian who
cares—and there are tens of thousands of him
in Russia and always will be—will look upon
that army of the Island Empire of the East as

his own rallying-point, his own line of first defence? Head-work and heart-work might do wonders toward the bringing of that day.

We are in this war to a finish. We mean to stay in it until we down the Boche and all he stands for. Shall we forever blunder on in Russia with the English-speaking propensity for error? Shall the German be the only one who acts with wisdom—Machiavellian wisdom sometimes, but none the less far-seeing—as to the attributes of strange peoples? The German has made more mistakes as an international student of racial psychology than we. True. But in the instances where he has shown wisdom let us learn from him. Let us teach the Russian. He is eager to learn, really, and his only school is either dominated by or wholesomely tinctured with German propaganda. We do not need to stoop to methods of lying fraud to compete with the Boche in Russia. The truth, the whole truth and nothing but the truth is the finest basis in the world for international educational work.

Let Japan go to Siberia—and let something else go with her.

Let us not only save the stores in Vladivostok, the Trans-Siberian Railway Line, and the products and territory of that vast region from the

Hun. Let us save the people of Siberia as well. Perhaps through that work we may gain ground further to the Westward, who knows?

Any work, however arduous, that bears even a remote promise of helping the Russian people to come into their own a little sooner, to check the disintegration of the vast land a moment earlier, to bring the dim light of the dawn of a newer, better day for Russia nearer, surer, is worth our every effort.

Let Japan go to Siberia. The ground is fallow. The seed of the righteousness of our cause will find sure root there. Let Japan go—and with her send the sowers.

FREDERIC COLEMAN.

CONTENTS

CHAPTER   PAGE

I   THE NEW JAPAN 15

II   JAPAN AND THE WAR 27

III   MORE ABOUT JAPAN 43

IV   CONCERNING SIBERIA 65

V   THE REVOLUTION COMES TO THE RUSSIAN FAR EAST 85

VI   NEW HANDS AT THE HELM OF GOVERNMENT 105

VII   ON DISCIPLINE 123

VIII   AGAREV—MAYOR OF VLADIVOSTOK . . 135

IX   THE TRANS-SIBERIAN TRANSPORTATION PROBLEM 161

X   THE FANATIC ELEMENT 183

XI   GERMAN PROPAGANDA 203

XII   BACK TO JAPAN—AND HOME TO THE U. S. A. 219

xi

THE NEW JAPAN

JAPAN OR GERMANY

CHAPTER I

THE NEW JAPAN

NINETY-NINE per cent of the Englishmen and Americans in the Orient have strong suspicions that when Japan moves her troops to any particular locality in the Far East, Japanese soldiers, Japanese influence and, very probably, Japanese jurisdiction will be cemented to that locality so tightly that a temporary expedient will drift in time into a permanent occupation.

A study of conditions in the Orient in 1916 and 1917 shows ample reason for an abandonment of such theories or at least a very wholesale alteration of them.

The fact that the wars which Japan has waged with foreign powers have been for her national security rather than for territorial aggrandisement, or at least that national security has been the leading factor in Japan's war policy, is a conclusion which clever students of Oriental affairs are becoming daily more willing to accept.

Japan's continual encroachments on the sovereignty of China, particularly in Manchuria, have very naturally obscured the real issue at times. A man who has seen and studied Japan's efforts to get a commercial foothold in Eastern Inner Mongolia cannot be blamed if he fails to see wherein the security of the Japanese Empire has necessitated some of the measures which Japan has allowed her officials and her nationals to adopt.

Nevertheless the underlying motive of Japan's policy to-day is fear. Japan is afraid of isolation. A certain number of Japanese jingoes write and talk continuously about Japan's greatness and her ability to press military domination. In no country in the world is there a greater difference between the loud-mouthed jingo of the nation and the sober, responsible statesman. On frequent occasions a series of articles in some paper of the comparative standing of the Tokio *Yamato* talk brazenly about the abrogation of the Anglo-Japanese treaty, or the forcing by Japan of America and Australia to change their laws in accordance with Japanese wishes. One of Japan's publicists frequently contributes an article to some magazine or review in Japan which, if taken seriously, would lead the reader to believe that not only was Japan's security thoroughly established, but that she was in a position to dictate to the other great powers as to whatever policy she decided to follow in the Far East.

People who read these things and from them judge Japan make a woful mistake. The most long-headed among the Japanese have long seen that Japan's position among the nations of the world required friendly co-operation and sympathy with some powers and actual alliance with others.

Russia's encroachments in the Far East prior to the Russo-Japanese war were actually a serious menace to Japan's security. Imperial Russia was a potential menace to Japan subsequent to the war which ended in 1905.

When, in the early part of this century, Count Hayashi in London brought off the Anglo-Japanese Alliance and made it the basis of Japan's foreign policy, he procured for Japan something that was so patent a necessity for the Island Empire of the East that it has been held by many students of Oriental affairs to have been, until the present war, a one-sided affair, very much to Japan's benefit.

While Japan has so arranged her railways that they ring 'round her rocky island coasts and are planned with every eye to their strategic value in time of possible warfare, the vital defence of Japan rests in her ability to keep open the sea routes which allow her to keep touch with the outside world. The fact that it is extremely unlikely, if not impossible, for any power to conduct a successful military operation on Japanese territory does not alter the fact that, should Japan be overwhelmed at sea and her islands surrounded by a hostile cordon of battleships and cruisers, her ultimate defeat would be certain.

In plain English, Japan's security has demanded for many years, and always will demand, an alliance with a power which is sufficiently strong at sea so that Japan will be freed from the danger of isolation.

A very brief study of Japan's history is required to show how gradually is coming the more general adoption in Japan—an adoption which is by no means general as yet—or the more statesmanlike and common-sense view of Japan's position internationally in contradistinction to the militarist and aggressive policy of those Japanese who have an inflated idea of Japan's importance and capacity.

The outcry of the Japanese press in 1915
against England and the almost universal criticism by Japan's newspapers of the Anglo-
Japanese Alliance was promulgated and fostered by the extreme militarist group. It was
one of the signs in 1915 of a last, dying effort
on the part of the old militarist element to as-
sert itself. Another of its expiring struggles
to impose its policies on the country was the
effort to force on to China the infamous Five
Group Demands.

In those days Japan's foreign policy was in
the hands of the Genro, or Elder Statesmen.
The Premier, Count Okuma, was a mere tool in
their hands. He and his Cabinet had no voice
in the foreign policy of Japan. A better element in Japan was coming to the fore. The
younger group of Japan's statesmen realised
the weakness of Japan's position. The Genro
were aged men; their lives were drawing to a
close. An increasing number of the thinkers of
Japan saw that when the Genro passed, a system and a policy would pass with them.

As the eyes of the Japanese began to open to
that situation, two schools took definite form:
one was the militarist school, which based its
ideas and theories upon German thought and
German teaching. As in Germany, the profes-

sor, scientist and publicist faction supplied
many advocates to the point of view held by the
militarists. The opposing school represented a
more liberal line of thought. It realised Japan's
weakness if isolation should be its portion—
whether that isolation would be military or economic. It saw that Japan's commercial future
in China was of vital necessity to Japan's successful development. The raw materials of the
Asiatic continent must be procured by Japan,
as she has insufficient mines of her own. Japan's manufactured products must be marketed
in China if she would continue the development
of her industries and commerce. China became
recognised as a necessity to Japan. Moreover,
the new school of thought realised that the only
possible method by which Japan's ideals could
be attained was by gaining the friendship of
China rather than its antagonism.

In October, 1916, when Count Terauchi became Premier, Japan was standing at the cross-
roads. Already those who had argued that Japan should follow the policy of Germany, were
meeting more and more opposition. Terauchi,
supposed to be militarist, pure and simple,
showed that he held many liberal ideas. He
declared at the outset that the policy of his
Government would be to coöperate unequivo-

cally with the Allies. He more than once displayed evidences that he conscientiously desired to live up to his obligations, so far as the war was concerned, and that so long as he was at the helm in Japan she could be depended upon to do so, at least to the extent of his power to guide his country and his countrymen.

Then came with 1917 the entrance of the United States into the war. America was no longer the great quiescent, dormant power on the other side of the Pacific, but was taking rapid steps toward becoming one of the strongest naval and military powers in the world. That change in Japan's great neighbour to the eastward put the final nails in the coffin of the policies of aggression advocated by Japan's extreme militarists. The only argument which they can bring to bear to-day against the liberal policies of New Japan is a croaking prophecy that Germany may be able to emerge victorious from the war. If Germany won, the element in Japan which has advocated that their country should follow in the footsteps of Germany would be undeniably strengthened. But even Japan, so far away from the conflict in Europe and so little informed as to the actual progress of events, is beginning to realise that Germany cannot win the war.

Japan is taking advantage, commercially and industrially, of the situation created in the Orient by the World War. She is leaving no stone unturned to gain a foothold wherever opportunity presents and is developing situations which she knows well may not exist for many years. This is particularly true of China. So long as Japan conducts her negotiations in the open, however, her crying need for Chinese raw material and her equal need of China as a market for her manufactured products give no little excuse to her efforts in that direction. She is again spurred by fear.

If she failed to take advantage of the absence of many of her competitors, she could never hope to successfully compete with them in certain lines and in certain localities. The desire on the part of Japan to push her commercial propaganda during the war almost assumes the character of a fevered rush for some newly discovered goldfield. She wants all the advantage she can get. She knows she is going to need it when the war is over and the great commercial and industrial nations turn their eyes to the Far East. She knows that she will need every advantage she has gained, and more, in the business war that is coming one day in the Orient. The advanced Japanese is under little hallucination as to the capability of most Japanese industrial concerns to hold their own on equal terms with the big manufacturers of America, England and Germany.

Just as her need for national security demands friendship and alliance with a group of great powers, so her ultimate industrial and economic welfare depends to a considerable extent on friendly relations with some of her most strenuous competitors.

JAPAN AND THE WAR

CHAPTER II

JAPAN AND THE WAR

WHEN I go to Japan I talk to many Japanese from many walks of life.

A sojourn in Japan before I went to Siberia and a stay of some weeks in Tokyo on my return journey filled my ears with arguments from the Japanese standpoint on the question of whether or not Japan should send her troops to Harbin, to Vladivostok, along the Trans-Siberian Railway as far west as Irkutsk, or even farther to the westward.

As all the world has discussed what England, France, and America think of such action by Japan, and the effect on the mind and temper of the Russian that would be the immediate result of a Japanese army on Siberian soil, the opinions and ideas of the Japanese themselves should not be left out of consideration.

I went to Siberia with the full knowledge that the Russians in the Pri-Amur country held very decided views about Japan. The Japanese were unpopular in the Russian Far East.

I discovered the extent of the feeling, its causes and how it has been fostered.

When I returned to Japan I was an advocate of Japanese troops, under certain circumstances, being sent to Harbin.

I lost no opportunity to get the right perspective in Tokyo. I left Yokohama for Vancouver with the confirmed belief that before the smart little soldiers of Japan's army were landed in Vladivostok or placed in the towns along the Trans-Siberian Railway the situation must be so serious that such action was recognised as inevitable. Conditions in Russia must needs first be well-nigh hopeless.

Of that, however, more anon. First, what did my friends in Japan think of all these things?

To begin with, my friends in Japan, with rare exceptions, were somewhat less interested in the war than you might think.

Japan went into the war without any rush of fine, high enthusiasm. The man in the street in Japan knew little about the whole business. The Government did it all. All Japan knew that the country had gone into the war out of loyalty to the Anglo-Japanese Alliance. But Japan was a long way from the fighting in Europe, and the fighting in the Orient,—the fighting with which the Japanese had to do,—was of little consequence, after all, and was soon over.

Japanese editors, of whom I know many, always reminded me of the restricted extent to which Japan had pledged her help. "Our war zone, it must be remembered," they would say, "is bounded on the west by the Indian Ocean. Read the terms of the Alliance and you will see that. Further to the west the British Government does not want us to go. We have always been told that our part in this war is to guard the Orient. We have done that. The sending of some of our fleet to the Mediterranean was an exception, and naturally was discussed as such by Japan. On all sides was criticism of the Government for taking such a step—every one wanted to know what reward Japan would get."

Sooner or later it comes to that in Japan, I'm afraid.

"What will we get out of it?" That question is at the back of all the arguments about the war. And naturally so, perhaps, in Japan.

This is a war, we say, for democracy. Japan is not a democracy. Count Terauchi, the able Premier of Japan, said not long ago that democracy is one of the greatest dangers of the age. Terauchi, whom I admire sincerely and who has proved himself to be a strong man indeed during the past year and a half, is no democrat. He might be an even stronger man if he was a democrat, but he could not, then, be Premier of Japan.

Thus, if Japan is not a democracy and wants none of democracy, so far as its own Government is concerned, why should the Japanese not look carefully into the possible gain that may come to them before they take a further step toward war—real. war, fighting and bloodshed and casualty and loss?

"We took Kiao-chow from the Germans, and our fleet not only convoyed the Australian troop-ships, but kept the Pacific clean of German raiders. Germany's islands in the Southern Seas, too, we occupied," said Mr. Tsushima to me one day. Mr. Tsushima is the editor of the Tokyo *Nichi Nichi,* which I have heard called the *Daily Mail* of Japan.

"You see, Japan has been doing everything in her power, seen and unseen, to assist the Allies," he continued. "Yet the Japanese are called selfish by many of you, because Japan has made a great economic advancement."

I confess I had called the Japanese selfish. They may have no monopoly of that virtue, but they are selfish. I had told Mr. Tsushima, further, that I thought Japan too indifferent to the war—that Japan did not pay the sort of serious attention to the war she should do.

"What would you have Japan do?" queried Mr. Tsushima. "Are the Western Allies in a round-about way urging Japan to mobilise her soldiers and send them to Europe?"

I admitted I could not say that. Pichon in France had long wanted the army of Japan on the Western Front, but few supporters of such a policy stood with him.

"Only a small section of Japanese favoured M. Pichon's proposal," continued Mr. Tsushima. "No general interest was aroused in Japan by it, but it always crops up when there is a reverse for the Entente in the war situation. I think no Japanese statesmen of common sense have considered the matter seriously. If the Entente armies reach a point where they really require reënforcement by the Japanese army, Japan may not shirk her duty, but before the Allies request Japan's mobilisation let them review the reasons why Japan joined in the war, and what material assistance she has rendered. Then let them make up their minds as to what Japan will gain."

He had reached the moot point at last. Most

of them come to it, in Japan, if you give them
time.

One of the most astute of Japan's political
leaders became very frank with me after dinner one evening. We were discussing the steel
embargo. America was stopping the shipment
of steel to Japan and Japan was very much
upset in consequence.

I held that Japan was not pulling her fair
share of the war-load. She could well release
much of her shipping to assist the Atlantic
freight fleets. She could, without entailing actual hardship in Japan, send ships where bot-
toms were badly needed by the Allies,—where
the shortage of ships was the most vital point
of weakness in the Allies' armour.

My Japanese friend commenced his argument
in reply with the keynote—What would Japan
gain? He asked me to put myself in the place
of the average Japanese—the man of average
intelligence. This is how he thought I would
then view the proposal that Japan should make
further sacrifice in the war: The Japanese
are not a popular race. If they are to believe
what they hear and what they read, Canadians,
Americans of the Pacific Coast, Australians,
and the English and Americans in the Far East
—in short, those of the English-speaking races

with whom they are in a sense neighbours and with whom they sometimes come in touch, are not imbued with love for the Japanese. Quite the contrary. Russians do not love the Japanese.

When the war ends, all agree that a great commercial struggle will commence in the Orient. A combination of interests may or may not be made between nations, but who will look after the interests of Japan? Who beside herself? Will friendly hands be stretched out to her to assist her industrially and commercially? Never. If combinations are made, they will not include Japan. She will have to fight alone. She is less powerful financially than her big competitors, too. She has less wealth, less industrial capacity as yet, less commercial ability. She is a baby in business with few years of experience of organised business effort or combined commercial action behind her.

What is her wisest course? To keep her ships and foster her growing industries? To increase as best she may and while she may her growing hold on the commerce of China, taking advantage of the absence of her competitors from many a field in which she has none too much time to gain great advantage before they return to fight her with better weapons and un-

deniable inherent advantages of more than one
kind? Or should Japan give freely her help
to the Allies, reduce her shipping fleets, hamper her export trade, cut down the raw material
that is coming in to feed her mills and factories?
For what? To beat Germany? Then what?
What of the aftermath? Will her sacrifice be
rewarded? How?

Do you catch the drift? Do you see the point
of view from the Japanese side? I did. I not
only saw it then, but I kept rubbing shoulders
with it all the time I was in Japan. The Oriental
is not usually so outspoken as my friend the
political leader. He camouflages. But he is no
more inscrutable than are many Western men.
When he has an idea in the back of his head,
a fundamental idea that sticks there and on
which his theories are based and his house of
argument and reasoning is built, it can be
found, usually, if one gets under the surface.

The same thing applied with relation to talk
about sending Japanese soldiers away from
Japan to fight for the Allied Cause. Japan has
had a habit of getting some *quid pro quo* when
she fights. Her war with China in 1894 found
her too young and weak to insist on the benefits
she craved. In 1900 she lost nothing in the
Peace Negotiations that followed the Boxer

Trouble in China. In 1904, when she defeated Russia, her ambitions were clipped somewhat by watchful Powers. Still, Japan has been gaining, gaining gradually. Formosa, Korea, the railway zone in Manchuria, and now Kiao-chow (not to mention other parts of China where she is gaining gradually, too), have fallen under her protecting mantle.

There is another small prospective gain that comes to mind in these days of tortured, dis-integrated, groaning Russia. Before the Great War, Manchuria, that province of China in which China has so little authority, was under a sort of dual protection. At the end of the Russo-Japanese war the Russians administered the Chinese Eastern Railway zone from Harbin south to Chang-chun. There Japanese admin-istration commenced, and ran down the railway to Mukden, then south to Port Arthur and Dai-ren, as well as eastward to Antung, on the road to Korea. The Japanese had worked hard to make the district along the railway productive. From Mukden north to Chang-chun the soya bean was being grown in increasing quantities. On to the north, from Chang-chun to Harbin, lay the most fertile lands of all. Not only along the railway but beside the River Sungari was untouched, virgin soil that Russian supervision

bade fair to leave untouched for all time. So
Japan began negotiations with Russia to extend her sphere of influence to Harbin, and
take over the administration of the railway
zone from Harbin south. The rights of navi-
gation on the upper reaches of the Sungari,
hitherto exclusively Russian, were also to go to
Japan.

I was in Tokyo in 1916 when Viscount Motono, now Minister of Foreign Affairs in the
Terauchi Government, came back from his position as Ambassador to Petrograd to take his
new folio. Before he left Russia he had tried
a diplomatic fall with his friends there. He
had won out. The bit of railway south of Harbin was to go to Japan. It was settled. Just
when the change was to be made I could not discover. After the war, surely, but possibly before. I imagined that the chaotic state of affairs in Russia toward the end of 1917 would
shelve all such deals indefinitely, but not long
ago in Peking, Baron Hayashi, Japan's able
Minister to China, told me he hoped the final
steps would shortly be taken whereby the transfer would be consummated.

Russian maladministration in Manchuria
will bear one sure result. Wherever Japan may
send her soldiers before the war is done, what-

ever reward she may expect or gain for the part she plays, her coveted line to Harbin will be hers inevitably and irrevocably. That will put her soldiers in Harbin, as railway guards, in such numbers as she deems necessary.

En passant, it won't be such a bad thing for the Manchurian farmer, after all. He will benefit all along that strip of railway from Harbin to Chang-chun, just as his brother agriculturalist has benefited further south. The Japanese farmer cannot compete with him. He is one of the best intensive farmers going, is the Manchurian. He can do more work and live more cheaply than any Japanese immigrant who may be induced to brave the rigours of the Manchurian climate. Few Japanese will come, and those who come will either drift back to the towns or go away. The Manchurian farmer is safe. It's disappointing in some ways, to some Japanese, but it can't be helped. The overflow population of Japan, if it finds it has to move out to make room for more overflow population some day, will not come to Manchuria—not in sufficient numbers to cut much figure.

While on the subject of the way Japan looks upon rewards for effort, I frequently discussed the question of the future of Tsing-tau.

The rights Germany enjoyed in Shan-tung

and her towns of Tsing-tau and Kiao-chow were appropriated by the Japanese when they defeated the Boche in China in 1914. Japan made a sort of an agreement to evacuate Tsing-tau and go home one day, but the document is open to many an interpretation and the man who hopes to live until Shan-tung is free of Japanese control is planning a longevity which would be as extraordinary as the evacuation itself.

Not long ago I probed into this subject with a Japanese gentleman of sufficiently high official standing so that I was placed under a promise not to give his name. He said that the declaration of war by China against Germany and the cancellation of all the treaties and agreements with Germany left China and Japan free to discuss the disposition of the rights Germany had enjoyed in Shan-tung until Japan took them over.

After Japan had taken possession of Tsing-tau and ousted the Germans, she made a treaty with China in which she agreed to take the question up with Germany at the Peace Conference which would follow the Great War, and subsequently tell China all about it. That is not the phraseology used, but a study of the documents brings one to that sort of feeling. China's declaration of war against Germany, then, accord-

ing to my official Japanese friend, rendered that
Chino-Japanese agreement null and void.

"What is going to happen?" I asked.

"We will make an altogether new treaty with
China about Shan-tung," was the reply.

"Will Japan leave Shan-tung?"

"I think not," he said frankly.

We smiled.

I knew, and he knew that I knew.   So why not
be frank?

MORE ABOUT JAPAN

CHAPTER III

More About Japan

In trying to get an idea of what the Japanese think of sending an army to Siberia, we must be fair to the hustling, clever little Oriental folk. It is easy to get the wrong impression of a nation, especially when the medium of conversation is so difficult as that between a Japanese and an American. Few people realise how hard it is to express our ideas in Japanese. If the best scholar in Japan translated an English article into Japanese and later the next-best scholar translated the same article back into English, the differences between the result and the original text would be many and probably vital.

The Japanese does not think as the Westerner does, of course. He not only has a different way of thinking, but his mental process halts frequently when he is considering big, outside questions.

In 1911 Prince Katsura started for Russia

on a world-tour. In Manchuria he was met by
Hsu-Shi-Chang, one of the most astute of Chinese politicians. Hsu-Shi-Chang asked the
Prince what he thought of the political outlook
in the Orient.

Prince Katsura is reported to have replied
laconically and with a shrug of his shoulders,
"Japan is no longer Japan of the Orient; she
is now concerned with world politics."

I think that is true—more true to-day than
ever before, but it does not mean that the people
of Japan have kept pace with her Government.
Maybe that is not necessary, but in the end the
people have to be considered a bit, even in
Japan. Public opinion does not cut much figure
in the Orient yet, but one or two instances have
been seen of new influences at work, and working effectually, at that.

In a country where over seventy per cent of
the schools are primary schools, and where the
boys and girls spend several years mastering
the alphabet, or what stands for it, a mental
equipment which gives full equality with his
prototype in America can hardly be asked fairly
of the Japanese. He is no fool, mind you. But
his education is, on some counts, weird. It's
very Japanese.

Ask a Japanese school-boy who invented the

telegraph, the telephone, or the gramophone. Ask him who discovered electricity. He will answer, if he thinks he knows, in ninety-nine cases out of a hundred by naming some Japanese. His idea of foreign countries is vague. Japan sees to it that her sons think a lot of Japan. There is good in that idea, but there may be some bad if it is carried too far.

In a country which has a constitution of a sort, the preamble of which says it is to be ruled by a line of Emperors unbroken, eternal, descended from Heaven, and that no power on earth is to change one minute phrase or clause of that constitution except the Emperor himself—a constitution that makes the Ministers of the Crown responsible solely to the Emperor, who appoints them and dismisses them at will —its world politics depend little on the ideas and opinions of the man in the street.

The voter in Japan is not much in evidence. Less than five per cent of the population have the franchise, though any man who pays taxes in a sum which is the equivalent of five dollars or thereabouts per year has a vote. A poor country? Yes. And at the same time the most heavily taxed people in proportion to their earned incomes of any people in the world. So it is natural enough that the Japanese should have a view of outside lands that is not always in the right perspective.

The people of Japan will learn. They have learned much in a short cycle. They are always learning. But democracy and anti-materialism do not mean much to them yet.

One of the editors of the *Asahi* called on me in Tokyo not long ago and we indulged in a lengthy chat about the fight for Constitutionalism in Japan. I had not many days before, in Karazawa, seen Mr. Ozaki, Ex-Minister of Justice in the Okuma Cabinet, who, with Viscount Kato, leader of what terms itself the Constitutionalist Party in Japan, heads the fight for Constitutionalism.

"Ozaki is no further along the road than when I saw him in 1916," I remarked. "What are you doing, you Constitutionalists? What chance have you to make headway? Are you getting anywhere? Do you see any hope for your projects?"

He talked long and earnestly. Boiled down, his remarks held nothing but this: One day, some day, they hoped to make the Emperor see that certain changes in the Constitution were of vital interest to Japan and for Japan's welfare. Then they might enlist the Emperor's sympathy in their cause, and gain his support for their

proposals. A campaign of education—the proletariat educating the Crown. Interesting.

Mr. Tukotomy of the Tokyo *Kokumin Shim-*
bun is a live man. He is a wise man, on some
counts, though his contemporaries will not
agree to that. His was the only paper in Japan
of any weight or standing that was behind
Count Terauchi when he was made Premier in
October, 1916. A conversation with Mr. Tukotomy is always bright. He represents a certain
line of thought in Japan that has some influence. Tukotomy's idea in the latter part of
1917 was that Japan and America should help
Russia only on condition that the great, strug-
gling Slav nation put its house in order. If
Russia adopted a Constitution and proceeded
under some stable form of government, Japan
and America should join hands and give what
succour they could; but for either country to
try to assist Russia until the internal complica-
tions were in better shape, would be, he thought,
interfering with Russia's domestic affairs.
Tokotomy has travelled extensively on the
Asiatic Continent, and knows well the anti-
Japanese feeling in certain breasts in Siberia.
He knows equally well what a hornet's nest
would be raised in the Russian Far East if

Japanese interference with Russian affairs had the appearance of being forced.

To send troops to Siberia, unless there was no other way out, seemed to Tokotomy, to judge from his editorials and remarks, to risk no inconsiderable asset in a growing feeling of friendship for Japan among the Russians.

The most influential paper in the commercial world in Tokyo is the *Chugwai Shogyo*. Its editor is Mr. Yanada. I had more than one talk with him, and found him most keen to help Russia, but anxious that no mistaken policy would undermine the commercial structure Japan had already begun to build in the way of increased trade with Siberia.

Suggestions along that line started me off among Japan's shipping magnates, several of whom I had met. Every one of them to whom I talked referred to the great danger of incurring Russian enmity.

"It is the Chinese question all over again," said one. "Our politicians make some move that seems to them to be a gain to us and we lose the sympathy and friendship of the Chinese. Boycotts of Japanese goods follow. The Chinese refuse or hesitate to buy anything that comes from Japan. Hatred of us and rancour against us are fomented on all sides, and it takes years of quiet spade-work to get back the ground we have lost.

"The best thing about the present Government is that it is trying hard to make good friends of the Chinese. If you want to sell goods to a man you are careful not to antagonise him. It's the same way in Russia, or in Siberia. If we send troops there it may cause us a set-back for years in building up a market there. It's a very good potential market, too, is Russia, and we are sure to reap much good from it. I hope nothing happens to make the Russians feel bitter against us. There is too much of that now."

The war? Oh, yes, there IS a war. But my friend the Japanese shipping magnate was not thinking so much of the war just then as of "Business as Usual," and more particularly, business rather more than usual after the war. But he is no exception as Japanese business men go. They never take the war into consideration when they start movements, or try to do so.

I was in Osaka in 1916 when the outcry was raised in the cotton industrial world of Japan at the British Embargo against the entry of Japanese cotton goods into Great Britain during the war. I heard the same sort of outcry in 1917 in Japan at the time of the American Steel Embargo. There was less outcry when the Japanese Government tried to get ships for the Allies, but though less noise was heard more pressure was brought to bear. Terauchi was powerless against the big shipping interests. How far he really wanted to go no man may know, but certain it is that he would have liked to have come much nearer meeting the requests of the Allies than he could do.

Big business is supposed to be very material. Big business in Japan lives up to its bad name in that regard. It is all material, every bit.

Dr. Soyeda of the *Hochi,* one of the most widely-read and influential daily newspapers in Tokyo, was very much against all suggestions that an armed Japanese force should be sent to Europe, when that proposal was made, for the very reason that he thought it quite possible that the day might come when Japan's army would have to check Germany's encroachment on the Orient by way of Siberia. He held that view strongly and for months elaborated it—although he, too, was chary of hurting the feelings of the Russians. He thought Japan should play her part, however, and give all assistance demanded of her, even to the despatch of troops to Siberia.

While I was in Japan an article that attracted some general attention was published over the signature of Dr. Takahashi Sakuye, who was formerly a director of the Legislative Bureau. A well-known reviewer in Japan described Dr. Takahashi as a representative Japanese, a scholar of wide knowledge, who had held one of the most important positions in the whole Japanese official hierarchy. "Dr. Takahashi's views were," said an authority on things Japanese, "expressed with an ability that was rare, and displayed a wide knowledge of affairs." His views gave an interesting insight into the not uncommon combination in Japan of extreme insularity with unbounded Imperialism.

As I met more than one publicist, professor or soldier in Japan who held the views—or most of them—that were put forward in Dr. Takahashi's symposium, the following summary of its salient features will give the concrete ideas of many prominent thinkers in Japan:

No disarmament scheme, even should a world concert of the Powers endorse it, would be acceptable to Japan. The peace of the Far East is in Japan's keeping, and she can only be sure of herself as custodian of and guardian over it so long as she keeps her sword bright and loose in the scabbard. Japan should have a place

among the world Powers, a voice at the Peace
Conference when it comes. More, Japan's voice
should, at that conference, be an equal one with
that of any great Power. In the settlement of
questions relating to the Far East and the
mastery of the Pacific, Japan's voice should not
only be equal, but predominant—should be
heard above that of her partners. Japan's part
in the war is by no means negligible. She is
keeping guard over the whole of the Pacific and
Indian Oceans and a large part of the continent
of Asia, so as to leave the Allies free to fight
the enemy elsewhere. Her fleet is in the Medi-
teranean. Japan should, the war over, keep
Kiao-chow and all Germany's possessions
among the Islands of the Pacific. That Japan
should have an entirely undisputed hegemony of
Eastern Asia and the Pacific Islands is an essen-
tial to that keeping the peace in the Orient
which is Japan's high mission among nations.
China must be protected. Japan may take over
Germany's rights there, but otherwise no encroachments on Chinese soil must be permitted,
least of all by Germany. If Germany obtained a
new port in China it would "make the present
war meaningless." For that matter, no country
should obtain any fresh hold on China, except
that Japan should hold what she won from the

More about Japan 53

enemy—that it happens to be on Chinese soil is a mere circumstance. China's affairs would be settled at the Peace Conference, but China's voice there would be a minor quantity. Always in the foreground is the thought of Japan's great sacrifices for China—her sacrifice in Manchuria when she fought Russia, her sacrifice in Kiao-chow when she fought Germany. That China did not ask Japan to fight in either instance, and that Japan, in each case, held what she had won, or hopes to do so, makes her efforts no less a sacrifice. She paid a price to free parts of China from the foreigner, and though China has just as little, or less, to say about these localities, and Japan's voice there has drowned out all other voices, that is all part of her great policy of keeping the peace of the Far East. It is the realisation of her duty, her mission as a nation, that leads Japan along such roads.

So much for Dr. Takahashi and his theories. Many a Japanese publicist stands with him on that platform. Many an influential, thinking Japanese considered in 1918 that should Japan's soldiers go to Siberia or to Russia to fight for the Allies, the peace of the Far East would demand many things which we Westerners would not connect with it. With the Takahashis to the fore, it would be easier to get the Japanese army into occupation of Far Eastern territory than out of it. And the Takahashis are not so negligible a quantity in Japanese life that we can afford to altogether forget them.

Among the army men in Japan the mere mention of the possibility that they might take part in the actual fighting was a tonic. They are more than keen to get into the war in real earnest.

A Japanese officer of high rank told me that he considered Japan's sending an army to Siberia would be the finest thing that could possibly happen to Japan, as he thought that such a step would be sure to eventually lead to the Japanese forces engaging the German army "somewhere further to the West."

"The other nations are becoming stronger, not weaker, by participation in the war," he said. "Only Russia is weaker, and she has lost her strength through abandoning the struggle. Japan will be stronger for fighting. Japan must, too, ever bear in mind that a maintenance of her military strength is as necessary to her as the breath of life to her people. What would Japan be without armies and armaments?

"Ours is an Island Empire. Do not forget that. We have too little raw material to suit us. To us, command of the sea is vital. If we should lose that to an enemy, our days as a Power would be numbered. We must not only maintain a strong navy, but we must continue to be allied to the strongest naval Power.

"Sea-control must be our first thought. America, Russia, even China, are stronger than we from the standpoint of actual territory and resources. We have beaten China. We have beaten Russia. We proved the value of our army. Had we not done so we could not have made the Alliance with Great Britain which is the rock on which the whole structure of our security is built. England would not have given us an Alliance which promised us the aid of the most powerful navy on the seas unless we had something to offer in return. We had our army. We could look after matters here in the Orient.

"We proved that, to some extent, at Kiao-chow. We must prove it further in Siberia, and in Russia, if necessary. Many Japanese talk about our trade with this country and with that as though it is a matter of life or death. So it may be. Much more serious to Japan than to other countries is the necessity of keeping open the lines over which must come to us those raw materials without which we could not wage war.''

The General took a book from his library shelf and read to me a few paragraphs from the pen of a noted publicist of the Japan of half a hundred years ago, one Hashimoto.

Hashimoto's argument was that Japan was too weak to stand by herself as an independent nation. He declared that Japan must develop herself in Korea, in Manchuria, in California and in some parts of China. The Ching Dynasty had such strength at that time in China that the Japanese expansion in that direction seemed blocked, so Hashimoto advised his country to look further west, toward India. Until the day Japan had, by permeating into such other lands, gained the benefit of trade and the supply of raw materials from them, Japan, Hashimoto averred, would never be really independent. In addition to this advice, Hashimoto advocated an Alliance with either England or Russia.

''That man was a seer,'' said the General. ''What he said fifty years ago holds good today. Japan must be friendly—must have Allies. Without them she is in a precarious position at once. We could always defend Japan from invasion, but oversea commerce is as necessary to our business life as the import of supplies is necessary to our military operations. Of what use would it be to us to be impregnable if we were stifled by some sea-power's hand on our trade arteries? It is plain we must have Allies. It is equally plain we must possess some asset to give them in return. We are that asset," he said, rising and striking his breast. "We—the army. We are strong and ready to fight. Russia is done. Germany will press for the Russian Far East, maybe, or at least she will strive to get the stores gathered there. We will keep Siberia from the Germans. We will keep the stores from the Germans. We want to do it. It is the justification of our very existence that we do it. It is vital that we play some part— something more, something greater than we have yet done. A blow struck by us at Germany in this war, is a blow struck for our own national security. My countrymen don't all see it that way, but it's plain enough, if you have your eyes open. I can see it."

So could I.

He was right—the General. And further, Count Terauchi himself would agree with every word the General had spoken.

Security. Japan fought two wars for it. Did she get it? She obtained temporary security.

Permanent security she can never have, except
at the cost of constant vigilance. Her policies
must be determined by that necessity for security. Never did Japan have a better chance
to cement her security a bit tighter than she
has to-day. I believe she sees that—her leaders
see it. She will act accordingly. Not for business and commercial gain only. Not for money,
though she is too poor a nation to leave pay-
ment of the bill out of account. But for security, first, last and all the time—that is the
motive that will drive Japan and is equally the
motive that will ensure that Japan will play
the game, cleanly, in the manner of a truly great
little Power.

Before I left Tokyo, I spoke, on Sunday afternoon, to several hundred Japanese students
at the Young Men's Christian Association. I
talked to them about the war, what it had meant
to the boys of France and of England, what it
was to mean in the very near future to hundreds
and thousands, one day to millions, of the boys
of America.

"I am genuinely sorry for the boys of Japan," I told them, "because Japan's armies are
not in the field. All the wonderful development
of character, all the splendid opportunities for
self-sacrifice, that the young manhood of the

Western world is reaping from the war-game is going to be missed by Japan, it seems Japan's boys would ripen and become men under that terrible test of fire through which the flower of the youth of France and England have passed. The old spirit of Bushido, the fierce loyalty to Emperor and country, the Spartan simplicity and clean, high spirit of the days of Old Japan would shine out in the young Japan of to-day, mellowed and enriched by something higher, something better, that comes sometimes to brave, young hearts fighting for a cause that contains no selfishness, no desire for gain or plunder or reward."

"This is a day of high ideals and clean intent," I told them. "The bigness of the game is beyond conception. It is so big it takes a boy and wraps him round until a light comes to his eyes, humble unit of the great whole that he feels himself to be, that is like the light that has shone in the eyes of crusaders and martyrs and patriots and heroes since the world began. It is only sacrifice and forgetfulness of self can put it there. The boys of the Western World are fighting for Humanity, for the Right and for God. It filters through careless young minds, filled with all the zest and fire of youth and gives them the touch that makes them great.

They all become heroes. They all become great. Would to God Japan's young manhood could feel the touch of that master-hand—what a day it would be for Japan."

When I had finished I went among the students, and chatted with some of them. One after another came to me, there and afterwards at my hotel and said that they felt the truth of what I had told them.

Sometimes a sudden hand clasp, sometimes the glint of a tear showed depth of emotion that words could not express. The boys of Japan, student boys, think deeply on such subjects, more deeply, perhaps, than most Japanese people realize.

One fine young fellow who talked long with me about the war said, "We are beginning to see that Japan has more at stake in this world-war than we knew. Japan has never really been in the war. We can learn enough from what we read about France and England to get that idea. Japan's heart is not in the war,—not yet. But is it not possible that the day may come when Japan will play a bigger part? Believe me, we boys would welcome it. We can see that the outcome of this war means all the difference to Japan—all the difference between going ahead and going back. Japan to-day stands divided between two schools. Years ago the old civilisation of Japan was condemned by the advanced school and a stampede was made to throw out things Japanese and adopt things Western in their stead. Naturally, materialism from the West came to us with the better elements of the new civilisation Japan was trying to absorb. The pendulum swung far, only to start back. A cult sprung up to save the old Japanese fashions and institutions. To-day Japan is puzzled. Her daily life is in a chaotic state. She is Japanese here and foreign there and often in a sad jumble in between. Her adoption of Western Civilisation has had a check. The war is on. It's a war between Liberalism and Militarism. In Japan there are Liberals and Militarists watching. The winning of the war by the Allies will mean almost as much to Japan and Japan's future progress as to that of any nation—perhaps more than to some. Western Civilisation, Japan thinks, is being tried, sorely tried. Will it stand the test? You can see, then, what it means to those of us who are sure Liberalism is right and Militarism is wrong. We are worried about the outcome. It means much to us. If we could only take a hand. If we could only help.''

Splendid boy! His words came from his heart. Who would not be glad, for the sake of him and his fellows, to see the Sun-Flag in the forefront of the fighting?

CONCERNING SIBERIA

CHAPTER IV

Concerning Siberia

WHAT has Japan done to better herself in Korea and Manchuria? She has developed Korea and worked great good there. She has brought no little agricultural prosperity to Manchuria. She has reached out to the North and practically concluded a deal with Russia, whereby her influence in Manchuria will shortly extend to Harbin, and include the finest district for the growing of the soya bean, the basis of the greatest industry in all Manchuria.

But while Japan is slowly developing Korea and Manchuria, a larger potential market lies in Siberia. Harbin, too, offers possibilities in itself. That the Japanese realise this can be judged from the fact that before the war there were very few Japanese in Harbin, but at the present time they are there in continually increasing numbers.

Japan's eyes have long been on the Russian Far East as a possible sphere of commercial development. Every opportunity was taken during the past few years to ship Japanese goods into Russia. Only Russia's dire necessity, however, ever allowed her to deal extensively with her former antagonist. The War of 1904-1905 was fought too far distant from Russia proper to take hold on the minds and imagination of the people of Western Russia to the extent to which it did among the Russian population in Siberia. The Japanese, since the Russo-Japanese War, have been feared and hated strenuously in the Russian Far East. Not one overt act can be laid to Japan's door during the present war which would in any way justify the feeling that permeates Siberia to the effect that Japan wishes to snap up the Pri-Amur.

That the Japanese would come to Siberia, aggressively, some day, was a statement I heard from many quarters in the Pri-Amur district. Up to the time of the revolution in Russia, and for many months afterwards, there was a comparatively satisfactory state of affairs existing throughout Siberia. The explanation of the more favourable conditions which prevailed in that region might be sought in Siberia's favourable economic position. There was no food shortage in Siberia worth taking into account.

Sugar had been hard to obtain at times, but otherwise no staple commodity had given out. Flour, vegetables and meat had always been fairly plentiful. Prices had risen very considerably. It was probably fair to say that the cost of living in some of the towns in Siberia was approximately double what it was before the war. On the other hand, wages had been generally higher and the working people had therefore never been seriously affected by the rise in the price of foodstuffs. The peasantry had pleanty of means of subsistence at hand and felt the war less than might have been thought. This condition of comparative security and prosperity had much to do with the failure of the extreme Socialist group to arouse full sympathy in the Russian Far East, when they came from Petrograd with their ultra-radical ideas and tried to implant them in Siberia. A population which is prosperous or which, at least, is not dogged by famine, is hardly likely to have any violent desire to upset the existing order of things. The Siberians seemed to me to be content with an orderly method of existence.

Siberia is a long way from Petrograd and Moscow. Its people are more independent and more developed politically than the people of

European Russia. Men in Eastern Siberia could always be found who could look upon the war dispassionately. They were far removed from it. They could, being used to greater freedom and a broader outlook, reason better for themselves and offer a firmer resistance to pernicious doctrines.

But to a man, they held that obsession about Japan. To understand it and appreciate it, one had to go into the history of the Government of Siberia before the present war.

When the news of the revolution in Petrograd in 1917 was flashed over the long line of wires that stretched across Siberia, to far Vladivostok and the seat of Government in Habarovsk, the Governor-General of the Pri-Amur was Nikolai L'vovitch Gondatti.

A study of this man and his influence as Governor-General of the Eastern part of Siberia throws many side-lights on the conditions that existed in the Far Northeast when the rule of the Romanoffs ended.

Nikolai Gondatti was a native of Moscow. Little is known of his parentage. He came of humble people—peasantry. Adopted in his early youth by a rich man, fortune favoured Gondatti with an education. From the outset he showed remarkable ability as a student. His

school days finished, he embarked on a career
as a teacher under the employment of the Immigration Department.

It was in this capacity that he first came to
Siberia.

He had not long been in the Far Northeast
before his ability allowed him to push his way
through the lower strata of officials. He was
an indefatigable worker and climbed rapidly.

Stolypin marked Gondatti as a useful subor-
dinate and later the young official became an un-
doubted favourite of Stolypin. To that astute
politician Gondatti owed much of his success in
official life.

As the years passed one rise after another
culminated in Gondatti's appointment to the
Governorship of Tomsk. This post suited him
and gave him opportunity for showing his growing capacity as an administrator. He became
noted for holding views of marked democratic
tendency, and as a politician gained followers
from the broad-minded standpoint with which
he viewed local and national affairs.

Then came the appointment of the Inter-de-
partmental commission, known as the Amur
Expedition. This was in 1910. This commission was composed of able men and much importance was placed upon its prospective work.

Gondatti was chosen as its president. This meant a year or two of work, in which he could show to the full advantage his knowledge of the Far Northeast and which, in turn, gave him opportunity for investigation which would make him the best-informed man in the world on the subject of Siberia.

The primary importance of the Amur Expedition was that the spirit behind it and the real object for which it was created were to lay the foundations for a fight in the Far East against Japan. This fight was to be a bloodless campaign, but was none the less carefully planned, nor was its importance to the Russians more negligible on that account.

Stolypin had always realised the fact that the only way that Russia could offset the development of Japan in Manchuria and prevent Japan's commercial encroachment north of Harbin, was to build up a solid Russian community in the Pri-Amur district. The power of Russia in the Far Northeast depended upon the success of Russia's colonisation schemes and projects for development in that part of the world.

The extent of the work of the Amur Expedition, which was guided by Gondatti's capable hand, covered every subject which could have a remote bearing on Russian progress. Not only questions of immigration and land settlement, but details as to agriculture and stockraising occupied much of the time of the commission. Every possible phase of prospective industries, a careful study of the geology of the district, as well as its botany, went hand in hand with investigations as to the development of transportation on land and water. The education and enlightenment of the people by means of schools and newspapers were given careful consideration. The subjects of shipping and fisheries were not forgotten.

The report of the Amur Expedition, in short, covers exhaustively and in detail practically every subject in which any one interested in Siberia might wish to delve.

Gondatti's personal characteristics were well suited to such work. He had a charming personality and carried himself with a simplicity that won those with whom he came into contact. His views became increasingly democratic, as he came into closer touch with the people, and there was no section of the population which he did not have an opportunity of studying at first hand.

At that time the Governor-General of the Pri-Amur was General Unterberger who had been either Governor or Governor-General of the district for more than a score of years. As might be imagined, General Unterberger was wedded to the old régime and was just pure bureaucrat to his finger-tips.

Before Gondatti's work on the Amur Expedition was concluded the more important men in the Far Northeast began to express the hope that he might be appointed successor to Unterberger, who had reached an age which made it sure that he would drift out of office not long thereafter.

Toward the end of 1911, Unterberger retired and the news came to Siberia that Gondatti had been made Governor-General in his place. There was universal rejoicing at this appointment. A positive enthusiasm swept over those whose hearts were in the work of developing the Russian Far East. These men felt that they were on the threshold of a new era. At last the old bureaucratic chains were to be knocked from the limbs of the strong young country and progress was to be assured. There was a universal confidence that under Gondatti's Governor-Generalship industries would be established, mining would be developed, railways would be built, waterways improved, the government of the country would be better organised, and the old faults of administration would be wiped out. New vigour and new life were infused into the community. Men who had struggled along under the impossible conditions which had obtained for so many years felt that a man who recognised the human element—a man who had himself come from the people— a man of marked democratic tendencies and of broad, sympathetic viewpoint—had come into power and that his very presence in the seat of authority gave sure promise of reform.

Alas for such hopes! In Gondatti's six years of office not one of them was realised. The day that saw the news reach Siberia of the overthrow of the Romanoffs in Petrograd found the Russian Far East in worse case than the day that marked the appointment of Gondatti as Governor-General. The story of that six years is one of those disappointing human documents which sometimes follow the placing of power in the hands of a promising but untried administrator. The job was too big for Gondatti. As Governor-General of the Pri-Amur he was a dismal, tragic failure.

For the first two or three years the better elements among the people in Siberia watched Gondatti's administration with amazement. He was always a hard worker and took the greatest

interest in his duties. He seemed to be genuinely devoted to the real progress of the country
and his personal ability showed itself unmis-
takably to those with whom he came into personal contact. No phase of the political situation, no detail as to the possible resources of
the country itself, no bit of information that
might give him a better insight into and grasp
of the problems with which he was confronted
could have been asked from him. He was a
storehouse of information and had a wonderful
memory. His charm of manner never failed
him, and he was always ready on public occasions as a speaker of marked ability. No one
came to him with a project into which he would
not go, and he was easy of access. With all
this, Gondatti was inherently a politician and
an office-seeker. He had been so from youth and
certain characteristics had moulded themselves
into his character in such a way as to detract
from his sincerity. Beneath all the smiling ex-
terior, in spite of the keen intellect with which
he had been endowed, he was a time-server and
given to using tools which were unworthy of
him.

During the latter part of his administration
his popularity waned; in fact, the pendulum
swung the other way. He became known as a

man who would promise anything, whether or not he had the intention of fulfilling his promise. He gained the name of a hypocrite. People who found no difficulty in reaching him and who were treated most charmingly by him, came away dissatisfied. He was looked upon with a general feeling of distrust. While he would talk democracy at length and with great freedom, his actions were declared to be undemocratic. Many of the old bureaucratic faults were allowed to remain in the administration. He was not above personal petty feuds. Here and there he showed spite in his dealings with those whom he did not like. Above all that led to the eventual dislike in which he was held by the people was the fact that his subordinates and mercenaries were the last class with whom he should have surrounded himself. Any means to obtain his ends seemed to be excused to him if he thought them the best medium toward a successful prosecution of his desires.

Stupid and dishonest officials thrived in some quarters under him. Never in the history of the Pri-Amur had the police been so utterly corrupt and so absolutely incompetent.

Thus his star, which had risen so rapidly and so brilliantly, began to wane as he was tried and found wanting. The pity of it was that

that star was, too, the star of the Russian Far East. The precious years went by. Opportunities that were never to be regained were lost. The genuine spirit of desire for co-operation and reorganisation of the great Far Northeast by Russia was sacrificed on the altar of Gondatti's personal ambition and mistaken policies. The man was too small for his task.

The peculiarity of this situation was rendered the more great from the fact that Gondatti started out in his career as Governor-General immensely popular with every class, and though his object in view was one with which all those about him were in sympathy—for all the people recognised Russia's necessities in this regard—he roused the actual antagonism of the vast majority of the people in the region.

The real root of the trouble, to be as charitable to Gondatti as possible, probably lay in the fact that he was incapable of realising that many of the reforms which he would have liked to effect could not be brought about so quickly as he wished. He moved too rapidly along certain lines, where the revolutionary character of his efforts proved their own undoing and at the same time failed signally to move with sufficient rapidity along many minor lines of reform, which his time-serving tendencies apparently prevented him from handling without gloves.

One attribute possessed by Gondatti has never been disputed. He was rabidly anti-Japanese. He left no stone unturned to block the Japanese wherever he could, and was ever fearful of their progress and advancement in the Far East. He resented bitterly any efforts of the Japanese to penetrate commercially into Siberia, and was ever at loggerheads with Japan over what he termed its unwarrantable interference with and encroachment upon Russian fishing interests.

A study of Gondatti's three pet projects, none of which were brought to a successful consummation, shows the general trend of Russian effort in the Far Northeast, and from them may be gained valuable lessons as regards the future of Siberia.

Gondatti's three attempted achievements were his effort to eliminate alien labour—with particular reference to the Chinese—his scheme for the deepening of the Amur Estuary, and his project for the imposition of a duty on imported wheat.

Gondatti was obsessed with the idea that the best way to develop Siberia was to shut out alien labour and thus increase the numbers of the Russian labouring population the more rap-

idly. Had Gondatti been somewhat more broad-
minded in his handling of this subject, he would
have realized that during the few years of his
Governor-Generalship he could do little more
than to start the elimination of alien labour and
that the continuation of such process must of
necessity go hand in hand with the growth of
the Russian population. To rob a community of
the great blessing of cheap and efficient labour,
particularly when no other sort of labour is at
hand to take its place, can have little other effect on the employer class throughout the community than to arouse in it a very deep sense
of antagonism. Throughout Siberia there is
hardly a class which did not view with suspicion
and disapproval Gondatti's plans to exclude
Chinese labour from the Pri-Amur district.
The exclusion was to apply to the Koreans as
well. That the employers of labour in the commercial community, and particularly the mine
owners, should be inconvenienced by this was
inevitable. Gondatti undoubtedly expected their
opposition. Curiously, however, the one class
of people with whom the scheme might have
been expected to have found favour was equally
opposed to it. The tillers of the soil throughout the Russian Far East, never very industrious themselves, had found they could use

Chinese and Koreans in cultivating the land,
and while so doing gain a respite from many
of the more arduous phases of agricultural industry, and yet make both ends meet. To take
from them the cheap labour which allowed them
to indulge a natural propensity for an easy-
going life, was to them anathema. Thus Gondatti found no sympathisers for the exclusion
of Chinese and Korean labour, and his insis-
tence upon it created a great deal of animosity
against his administration. When the war broke
out in 1914 the machinery for the exclusion of
alien labour in Siberia had not been completed
and Gondatti apparently decided to mark time,
so far as that project was concerned, until peace
had come again.

A large amount of Gondatti's time and en-
ergy was devoted to the most ambitious of his
proposed public works—the deepening of the
Tartar Straits. The town and Port of Niko-
laievsk would have undoubtedly benefitted had
Gondatti's scheme for the deepening of the
Straits been carried through, but such benefit
would have been obtained at a cost which was
out of all proportion. The credits that Gondatti obtained and the amount of money that
he wasted in this connection aroused much condemnation from engineering and business

sources, and some general suspicion as to whether or not the money expended was being done so without some ulterior reason behind the expenditure. It might be noted in passing that a practical way exists of utilising the Amur River as a waterway and connecting it with a seaport. This would embody the consideration of de Castries Bay as a port instead of Niko-laievsk, thus avoiding the Straits of Tartary and the lower Amur. A canal through the Zizzi Lakes prevents no engineering difficulties which are in the least insurmountable.

The third one of Gondatti's pet schemes was never put into operation. Had the European war not taken place Gondatti would undoubt-edly have forced it through. This scheme was a proposed duty to be levied on all wheat im-ported into Russia. The exact amount of the duty which Gondatti wished to impose was thirty kopecs per pood. The primary and fun-damental reason for this duty was stated by Gondatti to be the encouragement of agricul-ture in the Pri-Amur. It is difficult to find two men in Siberia who agree on the various phases of this question. The general division of the community for and against this measure was the adhesion to it and support of it by the agri-culturists and the venomous and bitter antagonism to it on the part of the milling interests. The exclusion of Manchurian grain from Siberia spelled ruin to some of the milling companies which had been formed for the express purpose of handling that particular trade. The milling industry is the foremost industry, and practically the sole extensive one, in Siberia.

Some people consider that the Pri-Amur would be a splendid place for the extensive raising of wheat; others condemn the country as being anything but rich from an agricultural standpoint and argue that crops are particularly liable to disease and to damage by flood. Be that as it may, the proposal seemed to create a greater measure of opposition among those who were antagonistic to it than the relative support it had gained from those with whom it found favour. It certainly added to Gondatti's unpopularity, and the distrust in which the Governor-General was held.

Such, then, was the general political condition in Far Eastern Russia when the news came to Siberia of the revolution in Petrograd.

Gondatti was in Vladivostok with General Nischenkoff, the Commander-in-Chief of the Russian forces in the Far East.

THE REVOLUTION COMES TO
THE RUSSIAN FAR EAST

CHAPTER V

The Revolution Comes to the Russian Far East

News of the revolution in Petrograd could hardly have been a great shock to any Russian. The Revolution of 1905 had followed the realisation on the part of the great mass of the Russian people that they had been betrayed by the manner in which the Russian-Japanese War had been waged and ended. It was only lack of cohesion and organisation, as well as lack of competent leaders, that prevented the Revolution in 1905 from developing into a much more serious affair for the Romanoff régime than it proved to be. Those who knew Russia well saw this and felt that another great betrayal had only to be followed by a national realisation of it, in order to start the fires of revolution afresh.

The day the message came to Vladivostok to the effect that the revolution had taken place, Gondatti called a council of the higher officials.

It was there decided to give the news to the public without delay. It was, perhaps, unfortunate for Gondatti that at the psychological moment he was absent from the seat of government in Habarovsk. He lost no time returning from Vladivostok, but before he could reach Habarovsk, mischief had been set afoot.

In the absence of both the Governor-General and the Commander-in-Chief of the forces, the extreme radical element in Habarovsk was given an opportunity to form a committee and assume authority.

Therefore, when Gondatti and General Nischenkoff reached Habarovsk they were at once arrested by the Revolutionary Committee and placed in the military prison. Gondatti's house was searched and every document and paper therein was subjected to a minute examination. All sorts of stories were spread about Siberia as to what was found in Gondatti's house. One report said that eleven poods of gold were secreted there. The basis for this story was that Gondatti's visits to the various mines in the district frequently resulted in his receipt of presents of specimen nuggets. The rumour started with some casual remark about these sample bits of the products of Siberian gold mines and grew into a weird story, from which one might gather that a huge store of gold had been found in Gondatti's house.

Another tale which was widely circulated was to the effect that a large amount of opium was found concealed on Gondatti's premises. This started tongues a-wagging everywhere. Some opium had been confiscated from smugglers a short time before the revolution and Gondatti was taking charge of it until it could be forwarded for the needs of the Russian Red Cross, but this fact was unknown to the average man in the community. Hundreds of other rumours, many of them absolutely groundless, flew from lip to lip, until the animosity toward Gondatti had become universal.

Petrograd, as soon as it learned that the Governor-General had been placed in prison, immediately ordered his release. The committee treated this communication from the revolutionary government with complete defiance. Instead of being released, Gondatti was transferred to the municipal jail and there given the treatment of a common criminal. All the time orders were coming from the new revolutionary government to Gondatti, directing him to remain at his post. The Habarovsk committee consigned such orders to the waste basket and Gondatti remained in jail. Such a condition of things existed for more than two months. At last Petrograd commenced demanding Gondatti's presence at the Capitol. These demands became insistent and the committee ultimately decided to despatch Gondatti to Petrograd. The manner of his going was in sad contrast to the way he had been welcomed as Governor-General so few years previously. The Habarovsk committee compelled him to go on foot to the railway station, and all the way from the jail the people crowded the streets and jeered at the former Governor-General and heaped insults upon him. The very men who should have felt the greatest sympathy for and gratitude to Gondatti, engineered the storm of passion that rose against him among the worst elements of the community. They even went so far as to gather together a mob of low moral and intellectual calibre to insure ill-treatment for the departing Governor-General, who was sent from Habarovsk under an armed guard and in a third-class compartment. He escaped with his life and with little else.

Little good did Gondatti ever do in Siberia, but he left behind him a deep-rooted suspicion of the Japanese and a well-fostered spirit of antagonism and dislike toward them. He had been most strongly opposed to the Japanese during his term of office and never lost an opportunity to thwart them. He frequently spoke publicly in an apprehensive vein of the results of the constant encroachments made by the Japanese upon the trade of the country.

It is astonishing how deep-rooted a feeling like the anti-Japanese sentiment in Siberia can become. The Russian is so quiet and peaceable, so little inclined to bother his head particularly about affairs which do not immediately concern him, that one hardly expects his likes and dislikes of a people outside his own environment to sway him. But the Japanese menace is very real to the people of the Pri-Amur. It is a country of rumour. Every day news would be spread of Japanese troops being in occupation at Harbin, or having been landed at Vladivostok. The most visionary sort of stories were always in the air. A Russian from Irkutsk told me his wife used the threat of a Japanese invasion to quiet the children.

That the revolutionary element, particularly the extreme radicals, were always suspicious of some encroachment on Siberian territory might be gathered from the fact that when Admiral Knight went to Vladivostok on the Flagship *Brooklyn, a* rumour was started that the

American Government was going to take over
the Trans-Siberian Railway. The most powerful and prominent Bolsheviki in Vladivostok
told more than one of us that he not only held
this opinion, but intended to promulgate it.
An astute member of the English-speaking community arranged that this firebrand should go
to lunch with Admiral Knight on board the
Brooklyn. The Russian had the courage of
his convictions and was as outspoken in the
Admiral's cabin as he had been in the headquarters of the Soldiers' and Workmen's Deputies. When Admiral Knight learned that the
belief was held by many of the Russians that
the coming of the *Brooklyn* was a sure presage
to American occupation of the railway, he
placed before the Russian extremist, without
any delay for special preparation, the exact
text of the cablegram from the Naval Department in Washington which had taken Admiral
Knight into Siberian waters with his ship. That
telegram could not have been better or more
diplomatically worded had the incident in Vladivostok been foreseen. It contained simple
enough instructions and gave as a reason for
the visit of the warship to Vladivostok the fact
that it was desired to demonstrate to the Russians the complete friendship for and sym-

pathy with them of the American Government.

There was no Japanese Admiral with a wisely worded cablegram from his Government to allay Russian suspicions in Siberia. For the matter of that, however the cablegram from Tokyo might have been worded, it would have had little effect in the way of soothing any suspicions that might have been aroused as to Japan's intentions.

The fear of Japan had a good effect on the extremists who had such predominant voice in the newly formed governmental committees in Habarovsk and Vladivostok. The more conservative elements in the community used that fear and played upon it. In Harbin particularly, wild action on the part of the Committee of Soldiers' and Workmen's Delegates was held in check more than once by a reminder that any serious breaches of the peace would result in the coming of Japanese troops from Manchuria within a few hours. Matters were quite bad enough in Harbin, but they would have been infinitely worse but for the proximity of available Japanese troops.

This fear of Japan was very much in evidence during the first months of the Russian Revolution. In Vladivostok, for instance, the imminence of a Japanese landing was in every mouth.

It was a blessing, for it instilled fear into the
unruly elements. It gave confidence to the provisional authorities, who soon recognised its
value, and played on it. It was, in fact, the
subject of the pious gratitude of the more timid
among the people, who saw in it a safeguard
against the worst elements in Siberia.

For months the Japanese fleet was universally
believed to be cruising just off the Siberian
Coast and details of its composition were passed
from lip to lip in awed whispers. When a small
Japanese training ship happened to call at
Vladivostok there was almost a panic. No one
could be prevailed upon to doubt that she was
in wireless communication with the Japanese
naval force outside and prepared to call it into
the port on the slightest excuse, such as an outbreak or riot, with a view to the immediate
military occupation of Vladivostok by the Japanese.

I talked with a number of Russians of several
classes about the possibility that Japan might
have to guard the accumulated stores in Vladivostok. Nowhere in Siberia did I find a Russian in favour of this. It was to discuss this
question that I walked one day over the wharves
of Vladivostok and along the paths that lead
around the shores of the bay, with two Rus-

sians who were among the most astute and powerful of the new element that had the reins of
Government in Vladivostok in its hands. They
were against Japanese intervention in any form.
To see over 600,000 tons of cargo piled promiscuously here and there is an experience.   An
inevitable amount of loss and damage had resulted from the lack of protection which had
been accorded to the goods. The limited amount
of warehouse space in Vladivostok had been supplemented by some 82,000 square feet of go-
downs, but the greater part of the material gathered had been piled in the open.

To walk through those piles on piles of indispensable materials, most of which had come
from Japan and America, made one feel that
some one ought to guard them if there was any
immediate danger of their falling into the hands
of the Germans.

To return to the story of how the Russian
Revolution came to Siberia, General Nischenkoff, the Commander-in-Chief, was taken, after
a few weeks' confinement in the military prison
at Habarovsk, to the borders of the Pri-Amur,
where he was released.   In his place the committee, which contained a number of soldier
members, elected a Colonel Vissotsky. Vissotsky was a colonel in the reserves and not in

the regular army. He had once been a banker
in Vladivostok and was held in little esteem—
in fact, the greater part of the business element
in Vladivostok considered him an out-and-out
scoundrel. He held the position of Commander-
in-Chief, however, until the Revolutionary Government in Petrograd sent General Hagondokoff
to take the position. Hagondokoff was once
Governor of the Amur province, and both he and
his Chief of Staff, Domanyeffsky, are capable
officers. Vissotsky was deposed from the position of Commander-in-Chief upon Hagondokoff's arrival, without any difficulty, as the former never enjoyed the confidence of either committee or army and had no real authority. When
he issued an order the army would consider it
and if they agreed with it, obey it; if not, they
would forget it.

While Habarovsk was the capital of the Pri-
Amur, the committee which had been formed
there and which had thrown the Governor-General and the Commander-in-Chief into jail and
had subsequently turned them out of Siberia,
was never recognised in Far Eastern Russia as
being in supreme control. A better group than
the committee in Habarovsk was the committee
in Vladivostok, and the fact that Vladivostok
was at the end of the trans-Siberian railway and

was the great seaport of the Far Northeast
made the Vladivostok committee of more real
importance than the Habarovsk committee.

The Russian is an easily governed person. He
is docile. He will go a long way to escape
trouble. Any committee that represents itself
as being the government of the moment finds
less difficulty in usurping the direction of affairs than it would find in most other countries.

The great difficulty which was immediately
felt in Siberia after the revolution in Russia was
the labour problem. This was all the more natural in view of the fact that the labour problem
in the Far Northeast has ever been in an unset-
tled, unsatisfactory state. Gondatti's efforts to
do away with Chinese and Korean labour and
the scarcity of Russian labour, together with
the fact that the Russian is not a particularly
efficient laboring man in the abstract, each had
a bearing on the troubles that were to ensue.
There was no real industry, as such, in the Pri-
Amur when the revolution came. The flour milling industry was the only one which had been
long established. Gold mining was confined to
the Zeya and Amgun valleys and had never
proved particularly remunerative. Gondatti's
schemes for the development of the other min-
eral resources of the Pri-Amur had never

reached anything like conclusion. One might almost say that, except for the gold mining and the mining of zinc at Tiutiukhe, there is no mining industry in Siberia as yet. Consequently, except for the conduct of the railway line and such ordinary local industries as may be found in every community where good-sized towns and cities exist, no sufficient industrial life was to be found in the country from which to create or support a good-sized and intelligent body of working men.

The fact that the soldiers and working men, such as they are, with all their limitations, took over the government at Vladivostok and did as well with it for a time as they did do, is a lesson in itself as to the possibilities of rule by the people. The effect on the whole Pri-Amur district of the attitude and actions of the Vladivostok committee was more far-reaching than that of the Habarovsk committee.

Those first days of the Russian revolution, with the continual contradictory orders that came to Vladivostok from Petrograd, and with that excess of zeal with which a new group in power feels its first strength, might have produced more sinister results.

The power in Vladivostok was in the hands, when the revolution came, of men who were known to be henchmen of Gondatti's.   The Governor-General at Vladivostok was named Tolmatchoff. When the government was taken over by a Committee of Public Safety—immediately formed on receipt of the news that the old regime had been superseded in Russia—Tolmatchoff was deprived of his official residence, with the exception of one bedroom. He was given to understand that his authority had been taken over by the committee, although the fact that he was a popular man and that the Committee of Public Safety itself was formed from quite rational elements, protected the Governor-General from any personal ill-treatment. Tolmatchoff wisely applied at once for leave of absence and until it was granted and he left for Petrograd, he kept quietly in the background and took no part in the conduct of public affairs.

The Vice-Governor of Vladivostok, Ternovsky, might have come into prominence at this point, except for the fact that he was a great favourite of Gondatti's. That alone proved his downfall. As in the instance of the Governor-General, there was no bitterness of feeling against him and he was not only allowed to remain in Vladivostok but was given an official position subsequently under the new regime.

Vladivostok's Mayor was General Yushtchenkoff. He, too, was known as one of Gondatti's men, although he cut little figure one way or the other, as he was a man of no marked individuality or ability. In spite of this fact, he had been in touch so long with various municipal elements in Vladivostok, that he was able to gain a hearing with the Committee of Public Safety and to induce them to include among their numbers some of the more moderate citizens. Yushtchenkoff hung on long enough to effect some real good in this connection. One of the results of the Mayor's influence was that the Committee of Public Safety which first grouped itself around the old Municipal Government gradually became disassociated from the municipality and allowed distinctly civic interests to be handled by a purely municipal body.

The situation in Vladivostok immediately after the outbreak of the revolution was, then, that the Committee of Public Safety took over the powers of the Governor-General, in spite of the fact that Petrograd gave him orders to continue in authority. Most of the officials in the Government service carried on their work in the same way that they had done, except that they took orders from the Committee instead of the Governor-General. That moderate ele-

ments were in the Committee was evident from
the fact that no disturbance occurred in Vladivostok and that law and order were very well
maintained. The very first few hours and days
of the revolution seemed to hold some menace
of unruly conditions to come, but a better condition of things continued and no little common
sense in administration was shown by the Committee.

Only one incident occurred which showed the
animus of the new governing power for some
of the old bureaucratic group. The chief of
the commercial port of Vladivostok was a Baron
Toube. A deep feeling against Germany existed in the community and considerable popular indignation was directed against Toube, on
account of his German name. Toube was undoubtedly a man of exceptional capability. He
cared nothing for the opinions of other people,
however, and was accustomed to running the
port to suit himself. His methods and man-
ners were high-handed.

When the revolution came the feeling against
Toube took the form of frequent threats against
his safety and accusations of all sorts of pro-
German actions on his part. Threats came to
him by telephone and by anonymous letters.
Feeling that his safety would be more assured,

he moved his residence to one of the tugs in
the Bay. That gave his enemies the chance
for which they had been waiting. An outcry
at once arose to the effect that Toube was planning to escape. His arrest followed the popular
clamour. The Committee of Public Safety had
made no other move of this kind and that it
felt that possible injustice had been done to
Baron Toube, might be gauged from the fact
that the Committee explained its action to be
due to a desire to protect Toube from the people. Dame Rumour immediately became busy.
Stories to the effect that Toube had manipulated
the unloading of cargoes in the port in such
manner that combustible materials had been
so stored as to invite fire, soon developed into
statements that goods had actually been destroyed by Toube in his effort to assist the
Germans. While his first incarceration had
been in the fortress, it soon became necessary
to transfer him to the common jail. A couple
of months afterwards, despite the fact that
many charges had been formed against him and
there was a strong feeling on the part of the
Vladivostok people that he should be brought
to trial for dereliction of duty, better counsels
prevailed. He was released on bail eventually
and allowed to leave Siberia for Russia.

Thus the revolutionary element took control of affairs of government in Siberia, and the individuals in whose hands the conduct of affairs had previously rested drifted out, one after another, and left the new element in entire control.

A bad administration had left the country in anything but a sound industrial condition and the work of a Russian settlement of the Far Northeast had been but begun. The resources of the country were hardly as yet tapped. The day of the Russian Far East could not as yet have been said to have reached its dawn.

NEW HANDS AT THE HELM OF
GOVERNMENT

CHAPTER VI

New Hands at the Helm of Government

The first Committee of Public Safety formed in Vladivostok contained a majority of men who were of decidedly moderate tendencies. This fact bore fruit in two directions. First, the actions of the Committee assumed an importance greater than that of any other of the revolutionary committees in the Russian Far East. Second, its initial political complexion was identified too closely to the system which had existed before the revolution to allow the Committee to escape the constant charge on the part of its critics of reactionary and bourgeois tendencies.

Gradually, as the revolution gained impetus in Russia and the Bolshevik crew gained more and more ascendency, the extreme element in the Committee of Public Safety in Vladivostok gained ground, until to-day the conservative element has become practically subordinated, if not eliminated. In its place there has sprung up, however, a semi-conservatism—a sort of

Minimalist group against the Maximalists, which have had the effect of giving some balance to the mind and deliberations of the committee.

For several months after the revolution came to Siberia, the Committee of Public Safety held the reins of government, and considering the circumstances under which it was compelled to operate and the personnel of its members, it is only fair to accord to it—during those early days—a considerable element of success as regarded the results of its working.

One example of its capability was with reference to the manner in which it grappled with the police problem. Under the old regime the police of Vladivostok were worse than useless. They were corrupt and a menace to the social order of things municipal. The Committee of Public Safety immediately replaced the police by a militia force. No one, however much they could criticise the militia, could argue that they were not an improvement on the old police force. The maintenance of good order cannot be placed solely to the credit of the militia, for all classes of the population desired peace and quiet, and their continual effort seconded well the efforts of the new force.

The revolution was not many days old when

the Council of Soldiers' and Workmen's Deputies was formed and took a prominent part in operations. It worked hand in hand with the Committee of Public Safety and some members of the former body were taken into the latter. The soldiers in Vladivostok during the early days of the revolution numbered about thirty thousand. There were few workmen, comparatively. The fact that industry in the Pri-Amur was undeveloped and that no one firm or establishment employed many men, except the Government Arsenal, made it inevitable that the soldiers should be predominant in the Council of Soldiers' and Workmen's Deputies.

The history of that Council in Vladivostok would read much the same as the history of similar committees in other parts of Russia. Immediately upon their formation they passed a resolution, declaring that the commandant of the fortress could issue no orders before first submitting them to the Council for approval. Their commanding officer was an old man and in bad health. He had little option or inclination to quarrel with the mandate of the Council. Fortunately for affairs in Vladivostok one or two young soldiers, who were eloquent speakers, gained the immediate ascendency over their comrades, and, still more fortunately, possessed

no small amount of common sense. These young
fellows held quite sound opinions, and, but for
comparatively few instances, the Council of Soldiers' and Workmen's Deputies, so far as its
decrees which had to do with the soldiers themselves were concerned, took but little action
that could be described as other than rational.
When the Council applied its power to the ar-
bitration or settlement of labour disputes, its
judgment, as might be expected, was less sound.
Chief among its labours, however, was the Council's effort to weed out dishonest practices and
corrupt methods from Russian officialdom. The
soldiers' committee was just as keen to detect
and punish crooked officials of the new regime
as it would have been to have hounded out corrupt functionaries of the old bureaucratic group.

Their own organisation came in for no little
attention at their hands and when it seemed
necessary that the militia should be assisted in
the maintenance of good order, the soldiers
showed themselves to be willing and ready to
give such help.

Their action along one line was somewhat
amusing and intensely distasteful to the official
element. The Council desired to have one of
its own representatives keep active touch with
all branches of the public service. The work

of the Customs Officials, the receipt and despatch of cargo, and questions relating to the
amount of accommodation for the storage of
goods and the amount of car space on the railways, were items which the Council of Soldiers' and Workmen's Deputies considered vital
points with which they should come into close
contact and upon which they should keep a vigi-
lant eye. The utter and extraordinary ignorance
of some of the soldiers who were thus appointed
to watch official operation of one department or
another produced several amusing situations.
The object of the Committee and of the men
themselves, however, was a good one, and productive of good in the main.

The bourgeoisie and official classes of the old
day in Siberia could apparently no more work
with the new element than water could be mixed
with wine. The evident sincerity of the soldiers
was entirely misunderstood by the better educated classes, who failed more deplorably than
one would have thought possible. In Siberia,
as in the rest of Russia, what might usually
be spoken of as the better element of the population has shown no initiative, no real patriotism, and, above all, an entire absence of courage. Nowhere more patently than in Vladivostok could the better element in the com-

munity have rendered more signal service and
sympathetic understanding of and honest en-
deavour to work with the Council of Soldiers'
and Workmen's Deputies. In some parts of Russia the suspicion with which the bourgeoisie
were looked upon by the extreme radical element made it seem impossible that any assistance could be given by them. In Vladivostok
this was not the case—at least during the early
days of the revolution. Those who remained
of the more wealthy and official classes in Vladivostok made their primary mistake in creating
an organisation of their own, which was known
as "The Alliance of Free Russia." They lacked
punch and strength and vim, however, and, although they held meetings at times, in no instance was there evidence of their having had
the slightest effect or influence upon the trend
of events. Their association was subsequently
disbanded and assimilated with the "Party of
National Freedom."

Early in the game the Government in Petrograd realised that it was necessary to supply
some one from the central government to try
to hold Siberia closer to the seat of affairs in
Russia. The first representative of the new
government to arrive in Vladivostok was a man
named Rusanoff, who was a deputy for the

Maritime Province of Vladivostok in the Imperial Duma. Rusanoff was appointed by Petrograd to be Commissioner for the Pri-Amur. While he had no great personal authority and no practical experience of administration, he had the advantage of thorough local knowledge and was known to be honest and broad-minded. Petrograd made a good selection when they put him at the head of affairs, but he was not strong enough to really take the reins. The Committee of Public Safety co-operated with him to a certain extent, but never considered that they should take their cue from him.

Another element that loomed large in the situation in Vladivostok was the naval force stationed there. The Russian fleet in the port consisted only of a half dozen torpedo boats and a few small auxiliary vessels. Several thousand sailors were quartered in the barracks, however, and attached to the arsenal. Trouble with the sailors might not have ensued except for the arrival, during the first month of the revolution, of three agitators from the Baltic fleet. These devils came to Vladivostok with trouble in their hearts. Then it was that the sober minds and good common sense of the Council of Soldiers' and Workmen's Deputies was most needed. The firebrands from the Bal-

tic counselled a wholesale massacre of officers.
The Soldiers' Deputies soon put a veto on this
project. The sailors insisted upon the removal
of the Vice-Admiral, who was Commander-in-
Chief of the Port, and of the Port Admiral also.
In the Vice-Admiral's place they elected a Lieutenant, and an engineer captain was given the
position of Port Admiral. Here again the influence of the Soldiers' Deputies was marked,
for the appointment of the two new officers were
sound appointments of good men and Petrograd found no difficulty in confirming them.

Russian naval officers, as is well known, have
themselves to thank for the attitude of the Russian sailor toward them. Brutality of officers
toward men was reduced to a fine art in the
Russian navy. Since the revolution the naval
officers in Vladivostok have shone in an unen-
viable light, evidently afraid that retribution
might be dealt out to them and if their own
hands were clean that the sins of other officers
in previous days might cause some punishment
to fall on their own heads. They have, except
in very rare instances, shown no adaptability
whatever to the new conditions. A close observer told me in Vladivostok that the naval
officers since the revolution, without exception,
either exhibited complete subserviency to the

men or that they sulked and tried by all possible means to avoid further service in the navy. The natural result of this was that the men, finding their demands met with no opposition, made the most absurd proposals. The Vice-Admiral's house, which stands on the main street of Vladivostok, was taken over by the sailors and turned into a club for their own use, and almost any hour of the day or night that one passed, one could see them playing billiards, their girl friends standing about as interested spectators. To make their club a success they demanded from the officers ten per cent of the officers' pay. This sum is devoted to the expenses of the club, and if the officers should by any chance venture therein they are driven forth with insult and abuse. Under no circumstances will the sailors obey orders to take the government transport, a fairly busy ship, to sea, except on the express condition that they will be able to return for Sundays and holidays. Should an officer be housed in an apartment that the sailors consider too large and luxurious for him they summarily evict him and compel him to live elsewhere.

While all these things sound very absurd and very lawless and are in themselves inexcusably outrageous from one standpoint, the practices of the officers of the Russian navy in the old Romanoff days explain the spirit behind them. In spite of these excesses the sailors maintained order amongst themselves in Vladivostok and were not slow to punish drunkenness and other offences committed by their comrades. Certain it is that they preserved an orderly demeanour in the streets. Always among the sailors can be found extreme anarchists and their following ebbs and flows in accordance with their individual ability to hold sway over their fellows. For the most part the sailors in Vladivostok were inclined to be loyal to the temporary government. They were incredibly lazy, but that is an attribute by no means unusual in Russians. I saw but few of them that could be characterised as slovenly or dirty.

The influence of the Soldiers' and Workmen's Council and its desire for clean administration might be gauged from what befell General Sagatovsky, who commanded the artillery of the port, appointed by the Soldiers' Deputies to succeed General Kriloff, who was the Commander-in-Chief at Vladivostok at the time of the revolution. In spite of the fact that General Sagatovsky was the nominee of the Soldiers' Deputies, he was not in the position of Commander-in-Chief many weeks before certain malpractices were discovered, which were traced to him. At once he was deposed and placed under arrest, where he was held for many long months.

The transition that the minds of the Russian soldiers in Vladivostok went through during the early days of the revolution was an interesting study in psychology. At first they seemed to be wrapped in a fine glow of enthusiasm. High ideals were not uncommonly expressed. They felt apparently a fierce flame of patriotism burning in their breasts. All were eager to do something to help the new cause. They chafed under a sense of helplessness, and disappointment that they could not do something immediately constructive to assist the progress of the revolution.

Then this first burst of enthusiasm died out. A wave of demoralisation swept over the army. Discipline went by the board. Their attitude was passive rather than active. They took no overt steps and were guilty of no specific actions by which they could be particularly condemned. They destroyed no property. They were sober as a rule and behaved themselves, but it seemed that they had reached the stage of "don't care." Their disorganisation was marked. Their personal appearance became dirty and slovenly. In short, they ceased to be soldiers and became a mere disorganised mob.

The poor fellows had no help from their officers. The average Russian officer of lower rank was a poor stick with no education and little intelligence. He rarely had any moral fibre whatever. He had not been trained to care for his men nor for their welfare and had been brutal to them if he pleased, without reproof from his superiors. The Russian officer naturally felt no little fear as how the Russian soldier was going to look upon him under the new conditions. Had the officers, as a class, been efficient and courageous, when confronted with the moral and psychological problem presented by the dying out of the soldiers' enthusiasm, they might have been a useful factor in the situation. As it was, they were worse than useless. Most of them seemed thoroughly cowed. I rarely met one and engaged in any kind of conversation with him that the predominant idea in his mind was not escape from Russia and the Russian army. I do not wish to throw too much blame upon him for this, for it was natural for the officers to wish to get away, but it is deplorable that they were not of better class, for in Siberia at least clever and conscientious work on their part, had they put heart into their efforts, would have resulted in a much better feeling between officers and men.

As the months passed, the third phase of the transition came on. It was to the credit of the men themselves that some sort of reformation seemed to be working and that it came from themselves—from within. This was solely due to the fact that in their own numbers there were some young fellows who possessed no little common sense and honesty of purpose. Discipline of a sort began to reassert itself. It was not the old discipline, which was born of fear of a heavy fist or a club. It was discipline that was being adopted by the men because some of the wiser of their own fellows had shown them that they were better off under discipline, and that they could not be soldiers without it. True, it didn't go very far. Nevertheless, it was a genuine movement and as such was interesting, even in its stages of inception. While the men did not salute their officers, they bore themselves quite differently to their superiors, and there seemed to be hope of the natural enmity that the soldiers had begun to have for the officers disappearing in time. One has to know the Russian army thoroughly to realise how much this meant. The poor Russian soldier has had little for which to live.

He has been a brave, hard fighter and no one has cared a rap whether he lived or died. What probably was brought home to him more forcibly was the fact that nobody cared whether he suffered while he was alive. To ask him to have any inherent respect or love for his superiors or to have any real fundamental appreciation of the value of discipline and order was out of the question. Therefore, when the soldiers in Vladivostok began to buck up, smarten themselves, and show by their general bearing that they were trying to be better soldiers, it was concrete evidence of the amount of good that can be done among that class of soldiers by a little missionary work on the part of those who know them and sympathise with them.

Some units among the soldiers of the Siberian army became imbued with a definite anarchistic view. Some regiments dismissed quite fairly competent officers and put utterly incompetent ones in their places. As a whole, however, the Russian soldiers in Siberia, and particularly in Vladivostok, were by no means anarchists. The anarchists in Vladivostok tried to get hold of the soldiers and started a definite propaganda with that end in view. A large anarchist manifestation was planned in Vladivostok, the date for it set, and threats made that on that occasion the reds would loot the offices of a paper which did not agree with their sentiments, would ransack and pillage some of the larger stores in the town and would arrest summarily the members of the Council of the Soldiers' and Workmen's Deputies.

The Council handled this matter splendidly. Trustworthy troops with machine guns were placed at various quarters about the city, and a broad smile illumined the faces of most of the men who had been so direly threatened. No effort was made to keep the anarchists from having their meeting, and have it they did. A number of them, including some soldiers, gathered together and indulged in some oratorical fireworks, but the lack of opposition and some possible foreboding that the quiet held some unknown menace of trouble to come in case they "started something," made them decide to abandon all idea of rioting and disperse peacefully when they had run out of adjectives, expletives and breath.

The net result of this meeting was that not only the anarchists but the rest of the soldiers, and the balance of the population of Vladivostok as well, realised that the extremists were but a small unimportant minority.

Thus may be pointed out the good that lies

in some of the soldier elements in Russia. There is plenty to criticise. It is perhaps little use to either condemn or excuse. The main point to be remembered is that the Russian soldier offers fine ground for missionary effort. He has a lovable personality and is easily swayed. He is not entirely unintelligent by any means, and while he has little to be patriotic about and has never been trained to be industrious, once he is convinced that a certain line of action is the right one to take, it is not difficult to get him to adopt it. He is strangely capable of enthusiasm for a project. He has always been abused and ill-treated, and since the revolution has been fed continuously and everlastingly on enough wicked and soulless propaganda to addle the brains of wiser men.

That the Council of Soldiers' and Workmen's Deputies which, after all, represent the thirty thousand soldiers in Vladivostok and which are a real power in the community, have co-operated with the Committee of Public Safety so well as they have done and with so little of bad result, is an encouraging feature rather than a discouraging one.

ON DISCIPLINE

CHAPTER VII

On Discipline

A junior officer of the Russian army who had
been promoted to a position of some importance
in Siberia, asked me to dinner one evening. We
had a long talk about army reorganisation in
Russia, and about the possibility of the Russian
soldier of this generation again absorbing any
ideas of discipline.

My young friend waxed eloquent in his denunciation of the type of Russian officer whose
attitude toward the Russian soldier for many,
many years was largely responsible for the result that no Russian soldier would be likely to
accord much respect or authority to a Russian
officer again for a long time to come.

My experience with the Russian army on different occasions gave me a groundwork for an
understanding of my young friend's feelings in
the matter. I remembered a day in China in
1900 during the Boxer troubles when I had gone
from Tientsin to Tongku for provender. We

were under heavy bombardment in Tientsin and supplies had run low. We drew lots to see which of our quartette of correspondents should journey down the Pei-ho and apply to some of the ships of the British fleet for permission to purchase eatables. The lot fell to me. The British officers on the men-of-war in Taku Bay were very hospitable and exceedingly kind. When I landed from a steam pinnace at Tongku on my return journey I was laden with a big sack of food and drink. I obtained assistance in carrying it to the railway station, which I reached just in time to catch the one train of the day for Tientsin.

We had not proceeded more than half of the 25-mile journey before the train came to a standstill and we were ordered out. The engine had stopped at a break in the line. A damaged bridge which the Chinese troops had destroyed was immediately in front of us, and far distant the smoke of another engine rose lazily in the quiet air. Nearly a mile away was the other section of the train for Tientsin and the passengers were already scurrying across the intervening ground. I managed to get my heavy load out of the compartment and on to the embankment in front of the engine. I tried to shoulder it before carrying it down the twelve or fifteen foot slope that led to the plain below. I realised that it was too heavy for me to carry to the Tientsin section of the train. I could not abandon it. It was worth almost its weight in gold to me at that moment. I turned to a member of the Russian railway company, which was hard at work repairing the damaged railway bridge in front of us, and noticing that he was idle for the moment, asked him in my most polite and best Russian if he would, for a consideration, assist me to carry my load across the break.

He was a strapping big fellow, that Russian soldier. He looked a strong man. Either he had gotten out of his bunk on the wrong side that morning or his breakfast had disagreed with him, for he not only refused to give me any assistance, but his refusal was couched in very abrupt terms.

He used an expression at the close of his brief remarks, which was not at all the sort of thing that he should have said to me. I stood and gazed at him for a moment, wondering what I could possibly have said which would have aroused in him the least feeling of antagonism. A hand fell on my shoulder and a Russian acquaintance, an officer of the staff who spoke good English, said to me, "What is the matter?'' I told him briefly. I explained that I had meant no harm in wanting to hire the Russian soldier to assist me.

"Did I hear that soldier use such-and-such an expression to you?" queried the officer.

"I don't know whether you did or not. I did," I replied.

The officer stepped a couple of paces forward and looked straight in the soldier's eyes. The latter's hand went to the vizor of his cap smartly, and remained in that position. Russian military discipline demanded that a soldier in the presence of an officer kept his hand at the salute until he had obtained the officer's permission to remove it. With some low exclamation of annoyance, the officer, doubling his fist, smashed the soldier squarely in the jaw. The poor fellow's heels were together, and the rail was immediately behind him. The blow was no light one and it was fair on the jaw. Over the soldier went, head over heels, down the bank, turning at least one complete somersault. Scrambling to his feet at the bottom of the slope he drew himself up and looked at the officer standing on the bank above. From the moment he was struck, during all his evolutions down the embankment, and again as he rose and looked up at the man who had struck him in

the face, his hand, so far as I could see, had
hardly once left the vizor of his cap. Russian
discipline.

When my young friend in Vladivostok talked
to me about the abuses to which Russian soldiers had been subjected for so many years, I
knew what he was talking about. One who has
been with the Russian army in the field in
time of war may not realise the extent to which
the Russian officer in time of peace exerted that
continual discipline, as he called it, which was
only another name for legalised brutality.

I was being rowed out from Port Arthur to
a big Russian man-of-war anchored in the harbour one day. I was seated on one side of the
coxswain, and on the other was an intelligent
and well born Russian officer of good rank. As
the sailors swung to their oars and the boat
shot across the blue waters of the harbour, the
question of discipline came under discussion. I
referred to the well-trained crew, whose smart-
ness seemed to me to be rather unusual in the
Russian navy, as I knew it. To illustrate just
what he meant by discipline, the officer turned
toward the coxswain who was on his left and,
half rising, struck the man full in the face with
his clenched fist. I winced as though I had
been the one struck. The sheer savagery of that

quick blow astounded me. The coxswain was a
fine type of man. He had a splendid face, and
he took the blow unflinchingly. The officers
hard jaw set, and as he saw the horror on my
face it goaded him to a further exhibition of
brutality. Again he struck—twice. The blood
ran down the face of the man at the tiller, but
he set his lips, and with his eyes straight ahead,
kept his hands on the tiller ropes.

I could stand it no longer, and told my Russian acquaintance plainly that such was the
case. When he saw that I had thoroughly lost
my temper, he regained his former sweet com-
posure, laughed, and taunted me with having a
soft heart. "You would not be one to teach
discipline in the Russian navy," he said, with
a sneer.

Such pictures come back to me sometimes
when I see Russian soldiers that refuse to salute their officers, and when there are evidences
that discipline has become lax, so far as the
recognition of authority goes among the Russian soldiers.

We had dinner, the young Russian officer and
me, with two others of the local Russian army
organisation. We dined in a private room. As
we were chatting after dinner, loud laughter
came through the folding doors which shut off

an adjoining room from ours. The boisterous
shouts from next door increased in volume, until they interrupted our conversation.

"Do you recognise the voice?" asked one of
the young officers of another. At that they all
listened and my friend rose, went to the door
and shouted through it, "I hope you're having
a good time, General." There was an answering shout from the next room, and after a few
exchanges of badinage through the closed door,
it was opened from the other side, and I saw
the gross form of a man in the uniform of a
Russian General seated on a sofa which had
been drawn a little way from the table. The
remains of what for Siberia must have been a
sumptuous repast were still in evidence. The
General's companions were not from the recognised social strata of the community. A
glance at them showed their walk in life. On
the table were bottles and glasses containing
some weird illicit sort of red liquor, undoubtedly alcoholic, and as such, prohibited by law. It
is seldom indeed that the law against the sale
of liquor is evaded in most restaurants and eat-
ing places in Siberia.

We were duly presented, and sat down for
coffee. Shortly afterwards we left the General with his disreputable associates, and

strolled off to our sleeping places. Mine was on the billiard room sofa of a hospitable friend. Beds were scarce in the town.

As we walked arm in arm through the rich moonlight, the clear, pure air striking us like a shower bath after the heated, polluted atmosphere of the close room, my young Russian friend took a long breath and said, "We were talking about Russian officers during dinner, were we not? That is the man we might be obeying to-day. We have put in his place a very young man who has had little military experience. It is not an enormously important position which he fills, and he is not a wonderfully capable fellow. He is a clean young man. He has some sense of responsibility as to his job. He has done nothing to disgrace his newly found rank. Of the two—the young soldier who has been placed, in spite of his lack of training, in command of his fellows, or the old soldier whom you saw to-night—which do you think the more likely to merit and receive respect at the hands of the men? If we have to salute an officer it had much better be a decent officer who has some self-respect. We have had too much of the other kind in the Russian army."

Something in that.

In 1912 I accompanied 126 officers—most of them picked staff officers—at their head the General in supreme command of all railway and other transportation for the Russian army—throughout the Russian Empire on a two-thousand-mile tour. We went into parts of Russia which were indeed the heart of it. More than one town we visited was primitive to a degree. In many places I was the first American the people had ever seen. The village and townsfolk, and the peasant people along the way were kind and hospitable. The country through which we passed was frequently interesting. Civic bodies in the larger places gave us lavish entertainment. Yet there was a sufficiency of drunkenness and debauchery among the Russian officers on that staff ride to make the observer wonder whether those who revelled in it were capable of serious effort. A capacity for drink and a freedom from all restraint were the chief characteristics of much too great a number of the officers of the Russian army of the old pre-war days.

When one thinks what the Russian soldier has undergone, when one realises the brutality from which he has suffered for decades, when it is taken into consideration that no Russian officer has been trained to take the slightest care for the welfare or comfort of his men, it is a surprise, that the Russian officers as a class have been molested so little by their men since the outbreak of the Russian revolution. The Russian officer has fought well in many instances. As a class, however, it can hardly be said that he merited much respect from his soldiers. After such a revulsion as the Russian revolution it was inevitable that he should be relegated in the minds of his soldiers to an entirely different position than that which he occupied under the old regime.

AGAREV—MAYOR OF VLADIVOSTOK

CHAPTER VIII

Agarev—Mayor of Vladivostok

The Committee of Public Safety in Vladivostok commenced to encounter, before the revolution was many months old, a new element of disturbance in the community. This was supplied by the fact that Vladivostok was the port at which the returning Russian political and criminal element flowed freely homeward from the United States, Canada and Australasia. Many men who came in with this immigration were good men. There was also a liberal scattering of some of the most thorough scoundrels that could be found. When the first contingents began to arrive, their coming was a unique event and one for which the townsfolk readily turned out. Every steamer from Japan brought a complement which, on landing, marched through the town with black flags bearing various inscriptions, headed by a band, singing on its way and halting at intervals for speeches.

An acquaintance of mine, who took particular

interest in these returning delegations, told me that there seemed to be a preponderance of Jews among these immigrants, but that they included exponents of every conceivable theory of government, misgovernment and anarchy. The early arrivals were greeted with enthusiasm, he said. Their speeches were listened to with attention and were doubtless productive of harm. But this sort of thing wears itself out in time. Wild-eyed enthusiasts spouting hare-brained propaganda can tire even Russian audiences. The day came when a less and less number of the townsfolk would turn out when the black flag processions came by. Women out shopping turned back to the bargain counter after a glance which was sufficient to show that it was the same old game over again. Workmen who had paused to watch and sometimes had followed some large contingent, shrugged their shoulders as the latest arrivals passed. Soldiers who had nothing else to do except listen to speeches became so accustomed to the reiteration of weird doctrines that they would not go across the street to hear new orators. First apathetic, the Vladivostok audiences became critical. Next they saw the humour of some of the speeches and would gather to be amused.

This feeling eventually changed, first to ridicule, and finally to open hostility.

The sailors in Vladivostok apparently decided that they could obtain considerable entertainment by interrupting some of the meetings. Soon the sailor element was recognised as being definitely in opposition to the returning prophets. Rough treatment began to be meted out to those whose speeches did not suit the sailors. A member of one group was so badly handled that he died of his injuries. News of this and similar occurrences somewhat abated the desire on the part of the returning orators to indulge in stump speaking in the streets of Vladivostok. The Soldiers' and Workmen's Deputies took the view that forcible measures were quite excusable if they were used to combat theories subversive of public order.

The general view was held, too, that among the returning immigrants was many a man in German pay. Certain it was that no one could have served Germany's cause any better whether or not they were on the payroll of the German secret service.

Invariable animosity was displayed against America by the agitators and political speakers who passed through Vladivostok on their way to Russia. That America was the home of plutocracy and despotism of wealth and that the American workingman was in worse case than any other workingman in the world was the burden of the song on the lips of most of the returning Russians who came from the United States. America's entrance into the war was declared by almost all of them to be purely in the interest of the plutocrats and the employers of labour and definitely against the interest of the American labouring classes.

Some mass meetings were ordered by the anarchists to take place in front of the American Consulate in Vladivostok. One in particular had as its chief motive the registering of a protest against the death sentence passed on Mooney in San Francisco. That Mooney and his accomplices should pay the extreme penalty of the law for the part he played in the dynamite outrage was to the extreme anarchist element a monstrous injustice. They intended to make great capital out of it. The speeches were planned to be particularly inflammatory and high feeling was anticipated. The gathering took place and without any outside suggestions whatever the whole matter was handled skilfully and beautifully by the Committee of Public Safety, assisted by the Council of Soldiers' and Workmen's Deputies. Cleverly, and without the slightest show of force, the meeting was shifted to an open spot at some distance from the American Consulate. When the speeches became too vividly anti-American, some mysterious soft pedal was applied and the phraseology of the speaker kept mysteriously within reasonable limits. Perfect order was maintained throughout. The American Consul was invited to attend and a copy of the resolution of the meeting, condemning the judicial proceedings in the Mooney case and demanding the release of the criminal, was handed to him. There the matter ended.

One of the reasons for the maintenance of a comparatively satisfactory state of affairs for so many months in Vladivostok was that there was little actual hardship in the community. Only people who have come into touch with hunger to the verge of starvation, or with exposure and cold to the danger of life, can realise what fertile ground is supplied for anarchistic doctrines and extremist propaganda by deprivation and suffering. Extreme conditions produce extremists. Food in Siberia has not been plentiful and the provisional government in Petrograd has interfered with the economic situation once or twice in a way that might have created some food shortage in Siberia; but no sufficient shortage occurred to cause real suffering. Laws which tamper with the monetary situation to a point which prevents Korean farmers from shipping live stock into Siberia means that the Vladivostok family must go without meat. Rules of railway commissions as regards the distribution of empty cars and short-sightedness as to coal shipments may result in a fuel shortage in Vladivostok, in spite of the fact that great coal deposits exist within easy reach under normal circumstances.

Further, the average man in Far Eastern Russia has reached a higher stage of individual development than his brother of Western Russia. Politically the people of Siberia and particularly the people of Vladivostok are far more independent, broad-minded and reasonable than in most parts of Russia. Anarchistic and other pernicious doctrines are considered visionary by a much larger proportion of the population in the east than in the west. Japan, too, is much closer to Vladivostok than Petrograd. The lessons of the Russo-Japanese war are much more vivid in the minds of the Russians of the Far East.

The first election for mayor that took place in Vladivostok in 1917 resulted in the selection of a man by the name of Agarev.

Some time afterwards I set out one morning in Vladivostok with the determination to pay a call on Agarev, the mayor. I had been told that Agarev had been in the United States, was a workman, and had wild ideas on the subject of Socialism.

Most of the people of the better classes in Vladivostok seemed to think that Agarev was just about as bad a man to have in the seat of authority as could be found.

I heard no good word for him on any side. One intelligent Russian told me that Agarev was a Leninist. Another told me that Agarev, if he could have his way, would divide up the property in Vladivostok at once. Still another told me that Agarev was crooked, that he would shortly find some way to line his own pockets, and that he was the sort of a man who was generally to be feared for his unscrupulousness.

Agarev had not been sufficiently long mayor of Vladivostok so that the foreign officials in the town had seen much of him. They were not rabid against him, but I suppose they were constantly hearing hard things said about him. At all events, it so happened that I had found no one who championed him.

I walked down Vladivostok's hilly main street until I came to the building which had been set aside as the seat of municipal government. The doorway was crowded with *tovarishchi*. All were comrades, readily enough. Everybody thereabouts was a comrade—a *tovarishchi*. The use of the word sometimes almost amounts to a passport, if one adopts the right tone and manner with it.

There was considerable bustle in the corridors. I stood for a moment in the hallway, watching the faces of the men who seemed to be doing business in that odd City Hall. It was a dirty place. The floor had been swept that morning, I should judge, but the walls were inconceivably grimy, and the windows had not had a washing for many a long day. Men in various walks of life had evidently been coopted into this new form of revolutionary government in Siberia. One could see intelligent faces pass at frequent intervals, and there was many a fine looking Russian standing in some group, for the large hallway was full of groups gathered here and there. One or two long haired enthusiasts with the stamp of the fanatic all over them rushed past, a bundle of papers in each hand. Most of the men who were hatless, thus distinguishing them from the casual visitor to the building, seemed sober and earnest about their work, and very attentive to it. I opened a door leading off the main corridor and stood for a moment watching a dozen clerks and assistants of some sort, each at his desk. They were working and working hard. Turning again into the corridor, I stepped to a soldier who stood by the foot of the stairs and asked him where I would find the mayor, Agarev.

While not actually impolite, the soldier made an apparently studied effort to assume a very careless independence, and implied by a jerk of the thumb over one shoulder that I would find the Worshipful Mayor somewhere up the stairway.

On the next landing there was more semblance of official order. Quite a crowd was waiting to see some one. Both men and women were gathered in little groups. One noticed the patience and quiet with which the Russian folk waited. There was conversation in plenty, but it was held in low tones, which sank still lower when some one approached or passed. Considering that these people were part and parcel of the proletariat, that the proletariat ruled thereabouts unquestionably, and that it was new to its feeling of power they seemed to me to be unusually humble.

I walked to a desk at which a soldier sat and tossed down my card, merely announcing that it was for Mr. Agarev. He picked it up, glanced at it quite stupidly, shook his head disparagingly, but lost no time in conveying it through the large door that opened to permit the entrance of only those who had permission to pass.

In a moment he had returned, and with a gesture motioned me to follow him. Arriving at another door he indicated it as the one of which I was in search, and left me standing outside, wondering whether to brazenly enter or announce my arrival with a modest knock.

Modesty not seeming a very necessary commodity at that juncture, I tried to assume the air of a *tovarishchi* and boldly entered. I found myself in a large waiting-room, a huge table in the centre, and great paintings about the walls, but not a soul in sight. Four doors led out of this large compartment, and I was apparently to be allowed to pursue my own investigations in my own way. Beginning with the right hand door, I opened it unceremoniously and there found, seated at a desk, and engaged in conversation with a man standing by him, a thoughtful, earnest-looking man of middle age. He rose and when I asked if he was the mayor, answered in broken English in the affirmative, and asked me to have a chair.

I spent an hour and a half in that office, and

I have seldom talked to a man who was more earnest and honest in voicing the opinions which he held than was Mayor Agarev of Vladivostok.

During the first part of our conversation we were subjected to constant interruptions. The unceremonious form of entrance which I had adopted seemed the rule, and not the exception. Men bent on serious official matters walked right into the room, and sometimes apologising and sometimes not, broke in on our conversation with a request to the mayor to give them an answer to some proposition or to glance over some document which they laid before him.

This annoyed me and Agarev seemed equally to dislike it. Smilingly, I suggested barring the door. The Mayor said there was no key. As the door opened inward, I conceived the idea of swinging a heavy oak centre table against it for a few moments. That made an effective barrier, particularly as I mounted it.

Sometimes it was hard to get Agarev's meaning, as my knowledge of Russian has ever been meagre and was suffering from long disuse. Agarev's English was simple and usually effective, but now and then he had to search for a word. He was earnest, however, in trying to transmit his ideas and was equally earnest in endeavouring to catch my meaning. Therefore,

we found no difficulty in gaining a very good
insight into what each of us thought on the
subject of democratic government, particularly
as applied to Siberia.

Agarev told me that he had been with the
Russian Purchasing Commission in America
during the early part of the war. He was a
mechanic and a clever one, and was used by
the Russian Commission as an expert in connection with mechanical matters. He told me
some interesting facts about the methods of
that Russian buying commission. Those facts
are not a part of this narrative, but the knowledge of them may have contributed to Agarev's
feeling that it would indeed be a bad form of
government which was not an improvement on
the Imperial Russian regime.

Agarev was not a well known man in Vladivostok. He had never seen the place before he
returned from the United States. He had run
for mayor on an open ticket and been elected
by a good majority. He was a Social Democrat
and an Internationalist. He belonged to the
left but not to the extreme left.

To see that man, a workman, an earnest fellow, leaning over his desk and trying to explain
to me the real meaning of the Russian revolution, would have brought conviction into the

heart of more than one sceptic as to the honesty of purpose which some of these Russian revolutionaries have brought to their task.

Agarev knew Lenin personally and liked him, but he told me that he by no means held with Lenin's views. He thought Lenin a fanatic and quite out of focus and perspective on some questions.

The idea that Agarev was anxious that I should absorb was that the real power of Russia was in the people. More than one hundred and twenty millions of Russians meant the revolution with their whole hearts and souls.

- Agarev's arraignment of the Government of the Czar, which, strangling Russia with its license and treachery, sold right and left her interests and those of her allies, was quite easy to understand. Agarev was one of those men who saw in that glare of liberty that illuminated the political horizon, hope for a more successful prosecution of the war, entailing the overthrow of German militarism. Agarev believed that the German people were strangled by the persecution of the Prussian junkers. Where Agarev differed from Lenin was in his attitude toward class war in Russia. Agarev thought that all Russians should pull together for the formulation of a new regime. The Maximalist theory

that the co-operation of the middle classes
should be denied and that the entire authority
of the country should be delivered into the
hands of revolutionary democracy was not ac-
cepted by Agarev in its entirety.

We discussed the class of people that made
up Siberia's citizenship. Agarev agreed that
a very large number of the local population
who were comparatively prosperous, industrious and intelligent, must be utilised in the general scheme of government which would have
to be formed.

He had already experienced some trouble with
the Maximalist element in Vladivostok. One or
two red-hot anarchists were working diligently
in the community and the mottoes that they ad-
vertised were very attractive. Their theories
found fertile soil in the uneducated masses, and
they were particularly active among the soldiers
and the workmen.

On the other hand, Agarev thought, the sober-
er element in the Russian Far East would prove
less liable to conversion to some of the more
wild ideas of the extreme left than might the
people of European Russia.

Agarev was against the continuance of the
war. He thought Russia had but little to gain
by going through a fourth winter campaign.

Still, he was no advocate of a peace which would assist Germany. He held the idea in common with so many of his compatriots that the German workingman would rise against the Kaiser.

Agarev was anxious that Americans should know that he and his class were conscientiously trying to evolve a form of government for Russia which would be fair and right to everybody. The keenness of the man, his simplicity, above all his ever-present earnestness, could not but strike a spark of sympathy in the heart of any man who listened to him. He talked long about the plans he had for civic government and improvement, and spoke of the difficulties which he found in the way. Unruly elements were always with him, around him, behind him. The Central Government in Petrograd sent out people at times whose ideas did not always fit in with the Agarevs. The labour question was becoming increasingly difficult. Workmen were demanding wages in excess of what employers thought they could pay. The workmen were cutting down the hours of labour to a minimum that made the sensible Agarev fearful of trouble. The more he talked about the labouring men the more his brow wrinkled. A look came into his eyes that showed that the problem loomed large in front of him and worried him.

We talked about the American railway material, the locomotives, the cars and the coal
trucks that were to come across the Pacific to
help solve the big problem of congested transportation on the Trans-Siberian Railway. I
spoke of the difficulties with which the railway
people would be faced when the workers tried to
take into their own hands the matter of erect-
ing these engines and cars. I spoke of the railway constructional work about Vladivostok
during the previous twelvemonth which had to
be abandoned, owing to the attitude of the labouring men. Agarev agreed that matters were
serious, but he was convinced, and his eyes lit
with a quiet fire as he said it, that there was
sufficiency of patriotism and love of their own
country in some Russian workmen still, to en-
able him to get together a nucleus around which
a considerable labour effort could be organised.

The general tone of Agarev's conversation
was that things were by no means hopeless. He
spoke often of his own incapacity and inexpe-
rience. He held no hallucinations on that subject. He was a workman. His associates were
for the most part workmen and soldiers. They
had to creep before they could walk. He knew
that some of his associates were incompetent,
but he considered they were all honest. He

wished to impress me with the fact that those who were trying to run the Government of the Pri-Amur District were doing so conscientiously, and not with any idea of personal gain or emolument.

We probed deeply into the question of what Siberia would do if the more sober element continued to have a voice in governmental affairs, while wilder, more revolutionary councils continued to prevail in Petrograd. That part of the conversation was mostly "ifs" and "buts." I gathered from it, nevertheless, that Agarev thought the extreme Bolsheviki element would find difficulty in carrying Siberia with it if it went too far.

Agarev realised the value of the friendship and sympathy of America and deplored the no inconsiderable amount of anti-American feeling among his associates. He was frank to say that he considered that there was much of plutocracy in America, and that it needed wiping out. He thought that the imperialism of England and the capitalistic control in France were menaces to sound international fellowship. Plainly, Agarev saw things to fight in Germany, things to fight in America, things to fight in England, and things to fight in France. It was hard to make him see that the method of fight-

ing these various conditions with which he and
his fellows disagreed must be a different method for each one. On that subject Agarev was
consistent—foolishly consistent. When I argued to him that the day of extreme plutocracy
in America was beginning to close; that the imperialism of England was to-day—so far as he
understood it to mean a policy of aggrandisement—a thing of the past, and that he was all
wrong about France, he listened most attentively.

I suggested that a campaign of education was
what was needed in America and England and
France, if it was true that the Russian proletariat was really further advanced than the people of those countries. When I pressed home
the argument that a campaign of education was
the only way for the internationalists to gain
ground, Agarev turned back to his contention
that what was needed against Germany, more
than the meagre resistance which might be
made against the German army by the scat-
tered and discouraged and disintegrated Russian legions, was a campaign of education to
convert the Teutonic labouring man.

On most subjects I could talk to my Russian
friends with the knowledge that they tried to get
my viewpoint. The one wall which I was always

finding across my path was the ingrained belief that Germany would some day rise against its ruling classes. I told Agarev that never until Russia had suffered all sorts of indignity at the hands of Germany—never until a German army had swept over defenceless Russia—would he or his fellows get the right perspective as to the mind of the German workingman. Educated in state schools, preached at in state churches, fed with state pap from infancy, the German workingman was utterly misread and is utterly misread by the Russian workingman. Germany has seen to that.

Agarev's summary of the situation politically in Russia was somewhat different than that which I encountered elsewhere. He drew up a little table for me, beginning with the Temporary Government and writing under that the Temporary Council of the Republic. Under that came the Central Administrative Committee, and then drawing a long line, he said, "These three are but the froth on the real power of Russia; the real power lies along this line below." He wrote three captions along that lower line: one was the Council of Workmen's and Soldiers' Deputies; next was the Central Committee of the Fleets, and the third was the Council of Peasant's Deputies.

"It has taken the outside world too long to realise that the real power in Russia lies in the hands of the people's committees," said Agarev. "The temporary government is, in a sense, only exploiting the real power of Russia. Temporary governments may come and go, but so long as there is a Russia, the power will be in the people. They may not know how to wield it. It may take them years to be able to express and organise that power. Dark days may be ahead, but the coming of a better day is sure."

Agarev told me that of all the political parties in Russia there were only half a dozen that cut much figure. He would divide all the political elements in Russia into two groups, the Internationalists and the Protectionists. On a writing pad he drew out his groups, placing the Internationalists on the left and the Protectionists on the right. The extreme right were the Cadets; next to them came the right section of the Socialist Revolutionaries. The third group of the Protectionist element was the right wing of the Social Democrats.

The left, the Internationalists, he divided into three groups likewise. The extreme left, the Bolsheviks, he said, were many of them Social Democrats, whose views were less extreme than people thought. Next in authority in Petrograd came the Maximalists, who were, according to Agarev, the left wing of the Socialist Revolutionaries. His third section of Internationalists was the left wing of the Social Democrats, which he termed Minimalists, and to which, I gathered, he belonged.

Agarev was satisfied that Lenin was not a traitor to Russia, nor bought with German gold. Agarev was against many of Lenin's policies.

The agitation that the Bolsheviki were carrying on against the Allies, did not get much sympathy in Siberia. At least, many Russians in Siberia were less rabid against the forms of government which the Allies enjoyed than were the Bolsheviki of European Russia. Another point of divergence between the extreme Bolshevik group and the Social Democrats of Siberia was the question of the complete socialisation of industrial concerns and the immediate confiscation of private property. While Agarev's views on these two points would be considered extremely radical, they were not anarchistic. He wanted to see a certain amount of nationalisation of big businesses, and he also wanted to see the land taken from the large land owners and the peasantry of the country given a chance to administer it. He would

reach neither goal, however, by hurried or unfair means. It was just those little differences,
,between the Bolshevik view in Russia and the
view of Agarev, those he represented and those
with whom he was grouped in Siberia, which
showed the difference between the Russian
point of view and the Siberian point of view.
It may have been hard sometimes to see the
actual difference, but it existed nevertheless and
was always cropping up.

I think that Agarev hoped some day to see
complete socialisation of industrial enterprises
in Russia. He was certainly very much in favour of an immediate peace, if an honourable
peace could be gained. His views on such topics
were not in accord with those of most of us
from the Western World, but his attitude toward them and toward us was such that friendly
co-operation and mutual understanding was by
no means impossible. The very fact that
Agarev and the best political elements in Siberia were tolerant of the idea that some one
beside the workingmen themselves might have
a voice in things to do with government and administration was a much more happy state of
affairs than one found in Petrograd or Moscow.

As we concluded our conversation, Agarev
stood beside me and said, "It is a big problem

for us and we are new to it. We want so much
to do right. We want so much to avoid making
mistakes. That we will never be able to do.
If you great people of America will give us
sympathy and assistance, if you will be patient
with us and try to understand us, if you will not
become angry and disgusted with us because
we make mistakes in the beginning, it will
help us wonderfully to pull through. We are
going to win in the end, in this generation or
the next, or possibly in some generation unborn.
There is too much good in Russia—it will not
be entirely lost."

Agarev took my hand in his, and I looked
straight into his clear, grey eyes,—patient eyes,
eyes that held in them some unconscious anticipation of trouble ahead. I felt a lump in my
throat as I tried to tell him that there are many
of us who sympathised but little with hosts of
his ideas and methods, but back of it all our
eyes were on a very similar goal, our hearts
were in a very similar fight.

I could not walk down the crowded stairway
and out into the bright sun and clear crisp air
of Vladivostok without a vague restless feeling
that trouble lay ahead for Agarev and his kind.
The Bolsheviki element with its catch phrases
was gaining the ear of the people. German

propaganda, hard at work in Siberia, as elsewhere, was assisting the overthrow of the Minimalist group, and the ultimate domination of
the Maximalists or even of the Bolsheviki.

But so long as there are men like Agarev,
who are fighting to save Siberia, no man can
withhold his sympathy, advice and such assistance as he may be able to give.

To what good end? God knows. Without
sympathy and assistance, without a word of
guidance here and a word of admonition there,
what good lies in such men and their work may
be irretrievably lost. Every atom of that good
which we can save, Russia needs—Siberia
needs. Who would withhold help, if there is
even a fighting chance that some of the seed
may take root and one day bear flower?

THE TRANS-SIBERIAN TRANS-PORTATION PROBLEM

CHAPTER IX

THE TRANS-SIBERIAN TRANSPORTATION PROBLEM

It is easy to criticise the actions of a man or a group as regards their handling of the affairs of the community. It is much more difficult to try to understand and appreciate the real fundamental reasons for the action of such people. To know just what the Committee of Public Safety, the Council of Soldiers' and Workmen's Deputies in Vladivostok and Mayor Agarev, with his assistants in the municipal government, might have been expected to have been able to effect in connection with their efforts toward a government of the people, by the people and for the people in the Pri-Amur, it is necessary to glance at the picture which Vladivostok and Siberia presented when the revolution in Petrograd drifted out across the Steppes and into the Russian Far East.

Never in the history of the country had it known decent constructive government. Was it to have any better form of government under the revolutionary regime? If not, if the most conscientious efforts on the part of a group of really honest citizens could not bring order out of chaos, were they more to be deserving of condemnation or of sympathy?

Let us first see the conditions which they had to face when they took upon themselves the task of untangling the ravelled skein of political affairs and the absolute chaos of economic conditions, into which the Far Northeast had been plunged.

Never since the completion of the Trans-Siberian Railway has its administration and operation been other than painfully inefficient.

The old bureaucratic Russia under the Romanoffs knew this well. Moreover, the bureaucrats knew the vital importance of the Trans-Siberian Railway to Russia in the great war that commenced in 1914, and no steps were taken to remedy a situation which must, by the very nature of things, have resulted sooner or later in an almost complete breakdown of the system.

Not only the general facts, but a great number of specific instances, may be cited to show that a pro-German element had a finger in the Trans-Siberian Railroad pie. All the disorganisation and all the delay was not to be put solely upon incompetency. Sometimes the sinister hand of some German operator behind the scenes might be discovered pulling wires that made the transportation of goods from Siberia to Russia more and more impossible as the war went on.

In spite of the fact that the administration of the Trans-Siberian road was inherently faulty during the first eighteen months of the war, the Siberian railway system, as a whole, proved more adequate to the demands that had been put upon it than one who knew the system might have anticipated.

The Russian railway employé of certain grades is by no means a bad railway man. The better type of railroad employé was working hard to try to achieve the maximum possible, and his efforts bore fruit.

Early in 1915 the immense amount of goods that were shipped to Vladivostok resulted in some congestion there. Efficient and capable local officials grappled with the trouble in a bold manner and in spite of Petrograd, rather than with its assistance, succeeded in temporarily cleaning up the difficulty.

When 1916 came, however, a very difficult situation had to be faced. In January of that year the railway was working at very high pressure. Its full capacity at that time allowed two hundred cars, carrying one thousand poods each, of through traffic goods to leave Vladivostok each day, in addition to which, in some of the early months of 1916 one hundred wagons left Vladivostok daily loaded with railway material.

Of the two hundred cars which left for the West daily, one hundred and sixty were set aside for goods and materials which were the property of the government, leaving a remaining forty for the goods of private firms and shippers.

This distinction between government goods and the goods of business houses was not an important one, for the reason that the latter included metals, machinery, leather, rubber, tanning extract, chemicals and such commodities which were, for the most part, consigned to factories which were busy with government work or to indispensable industries.

Vladivostok has had dumped upon it, since the beginning of the war, an amount of cargo far in excess of the capacity of the port, but the proportion of the material which could be described as useless toward the prosecution of the war is a negligible quantity. Few luxuries or articles that were not necessary to the life of the nation or the life of the people have passed over the Trans-Siberian Railway during the World War.

The end of January, 1916, saw the beginning of a congestion in the Port of Vladivostok which was to reach proportions beyond the imagination of any one in Siberia. At that time exclusive of government materials, some sixteen thousand tons of privately owned goods had been gathered in the port, mostly consisting of tea and cotton. No sooner had the spring of 1916 opened than the steamers began to crowd the quays and anchorages all about. They came laden for the most part with cotton, saltpetre, powder and barbed wire. The last day of February saw the government goods still moving out of Vladivostok toward the West, but the privately owned goods were piling up fast and warehouse accommodation was soon threatened.

During March the last of the go-down space was filled. First cotton, then gunnies, then rubber in great quantities began to be stored in the open. There was no other place to put it. Mid-March saw fifty thousand tons of private cargo safely landed but with no prospect of being shipped over the railway. By the 1st of June there were eighty thousand tons of private cargo and much more of government goods. The amount grew steadily until the early part of 1917, when there was a slight temporary diminution in the tonnage.

All this time the government cargo was being handled in some sort of way, although the number of the freight cars available was steadily dropping. In June, metals, lathes and Red Cross materials were piled high on the quayside and in the fields adjacent to the warehouses. Then came July with conditions growing worse daily.

The top had to be reached some time. Shipping was diverted and ordered stopped, but not before 674,000 tons of cargo was piled promiscuously here and there in the open spaces, and the fields around the Port of Vladivostok. Small imports cut this down in the latter part of 1917 and the work of the Stevens Railway Commission resulted in an increase of efficiency on the part of the railway service, which cleared up a proportion of the goods but the greater part of them still lie in Vladivostok to-day.

An inspection of the piles of goods and materials showed that an inevitable amount of loss and damage had resulted from the lack of protection which had been accorded the cargoes.

Railway material, nitrate of soda, barbed wire, tea, phosphates and munitions caused the greatest congestion. Next came metals, rice, cotton, machines and lathes, tanning extract, oils, rubber, tallow, gunnies and motor cars. It was pitiable to walk through those piles on piles of indispensable materials. The rolling stock of the railway had been allowed to get into disrepair to an extent which made it certain that until the results of the recommendations of the Stevens Commission were felt—long months in the future—the available freight capacity would continue to be miserably inadequate.

It was inevitable that the state of things which existed in Vladivostok should have resulted in strenuous efforts on the part of interested parties to obtain preference of the shipment of the goods in which they were interested. Up to the end of 1916 the heads of the government departments and the Commandant of the Fortress of Vladivostok had control of the disposal of the railway wagons. Working as a committee they were guided by general instructions received from Petrograd, but full power as to the allotment of space was left in local hands. The forty cars daily which were set aside for private cargo were jealously watched, the Vladivostok Chamber of Commerce assisting the committee with its allot-

ments. No favouritism, or at least very little,
existed.

The difficulties increased when toward the
autumn of 1916 the forty cars daily were reduced to twenty-five cars or less. Siberian merchants found themselves in a critical position.
Most of them sought to pull wires of every
sort to obtain car space. The usual method of
gaining an advantage over a competitor was to
conspire with minor railway officials. Go-be-
tweens, rumour said, coined money in connection with such transactions. The Russian authorities made no little effort to catch offend-
ers, but without any noticeable success. Every
one knew that crooked work was the rule rather
than the exception. One of the favourite de-
vices of the merchants was to arrange with the
railway employés to load unauthorised cargo
at wayside stations in the vicinity of Vladivostok. Another common practice was for the
merchant to obtain orders for forwarding a certain class of goods and despatch others in their
place. Unutilised space in freight cars which
contained bulky goods was snapped up with
avidity.

This condition of things went on for months
and was ample evidence of a bad organisation,
both of the police in Vladivostok and the rail-

way company itself. The rectification of abuses was continually proposed but never carried into effect. As regarded the prosecution of the war, the question of whether a private cargo or government cargo was forwarded was not of the greatest importance, however. When the total tonnage of goods shipped was taken into consideration, the amount of cargo that found its way over the railway was almost without exception destined for indispensable industries. Russia needed the goods, whether they were the property of the government or of outside firms.

At the end of December, 1916, an order came from Petrograd to Vladivostok that all wagons available should be utilised for the shipment of government materials. No other goods were to be forwarded unless a "naryad"—a despatch order—from Petrograd had been obtained. Two months before orders had come from Petrograd closing the Port of Vladivostok to private cargo unless it was shipped under special permits. Had this order been religiously obeyed—it was dated October 29th, 1916—a good end would have been served. For some reason it was not put into execution for months. Most of the private cargo that came in, if not all of it, subsequent to the issuance of this decree, came from Japan. Some feeling was caused in the Orient by the fact that the business houses of most of the Allies recognised that a difficult situation had arisen and co-operated to the fullest extent to assist. The Japanese were more interested in the profits that might be obtained than in assisting the Russian situation. This applied to the Japanese houses rather than to the Japanese government, which had always shown an inclination to play the game with Russia in the Far East during the war.

The coming of the Stevens Commission from America was the only ray of light on a very black horizon. The situation which was found by the American railway men was not hopeful.

First, the Siberian Railway was wasteful and inefficient in almost every particular. Never in peace times was rolling stock on the railway handled in the best way, and during the war the administration had become increasingly worse. While the government at Petrograd was inclined to blame Vladivostok to some extent for the congestion of the railway, it was not the inadequacy of the Port of Vladivostok itself which had been the primary cause of the trouble. Only a slight investigation was necessary to prove that ships that had come to

Vladivostok had fairly good despatch all through, until those days had come when the railway had broken down and the ships continued to arrive in increasing numbers.

That no covered accommodation existed for the cargoes, that no tarpaulins were to be had, that goods had to be piled promiscuously on the quays, in the fields by the water's edge and all over the hillsides adjacent to the coast, that the ground all about the basin of the bay became strewn with all manner of stuff, that loaded lighters were untouched for weeks and that steamers which after a long fight gained a berth alongside the quay could find no open place on which to deliver goods from their slings was the result of circumstances with which Vladivostok could not be expected to cope. There was little at fault so far as Vladivostok was concerned.

The Stevens Commission probed quickly to the heart of the matter and in very short time found the sore. It was not at Vladivostok.

Against the good working of the Siberian Railway stood the fundamental fact that the long line from Petrograd to Vladivostok—over 5,500 miles—was made up of five separate railways, each of which had its own independent administration and its own headquarters in

Petrograd. This division of control had never been properly co-ordinated and overlapping was continuous. Each section was interested in itself only and had nothing to do with the other four sections.

The Chinese Eastern Railway was not badly handled. The part of the line from Vladivostok to Tchita, while it might be improved, was capable of much better work as it stood than were some other parts of the line. The weakest point of all was the Tomsk Railway. From the very beginning it had been absolutely unable to cope with the demand. In the centre of the great trans-continental system, its weakness was the weakness of the whole line. From the commencement of the war every head of the railway department in Petrograd must have known how rotten the Tomsk railway administration had become and he must have known too of the vital importance of the whole system to the conduct of the war. Yet examination of the orders issued by the Minister of Ways and Communications shows that they were so hopelessly bureaucratic that no prospect of reform was evident.

As an example of the manner in which this Minister made fatal errors, the coal traffic through Siberia into Russia had gone from east to west. With coal in plentiful quantities at various points along the line there was absolutely no excuse for this. Coal should have come from west to east in the empty wagons that were being hurried back to Vladivostok to come westward again loaded with war material.

The apparent keynote of the trouble on the Trans-Siberian Railway was shortage of railway wagons, locomotives and general railway rolling stock. Repair had been hampered since the beginning of the war and all railway property had gotten into a deplorable state. The first cars to come to Siberia from America were ordered by the Russian Commission before the arrival of the Stevens Commission in Russia. The Russian Commission had ordered less than two hundred engines and cars, but the demand for more was so evident at the outset that before the Stevens Commission reached Russia, it ordered the construction of three times the number of engines and ten times the number of cars that had been ordered by the Russian Commission. Even this amount of rolling stock was only a drop in the bucket. The Russian railway people at Vladivostok expected that the arrival of this rolling stock from America under the orders placed in 1915, would be

followed immediately by further consignments
of wagons and locomotives. Further they
never dreamed that so few freight cars would
come back to them from Russia. That men in
charge in Vladivostok were able to grasp the
new situation and struggle strenuously with it
was shown by the fact that when it became
known in Siberia that the order for cars and
engines to be built in America had not been
supplemented by further orders and would not
be until the Stevens Commission had investi-
gated the matter at first hand, warehouses were
at once started. In December, 1916, the Vladivostok authorities decided to build 82,000 square
yards of new go-downs. This was too late, of
course, to save some of the cargo from damage, but the work was proceeded with boldly
and with considerable success. The work that
has actually been performed in Vladivostok,
considering the situation into which the officials
there were thrust, reflects credit on those who
had a hand in the job.

It was strange, indeed, that no fires of mag-
nitude took place, when so many combustible
piles of goods were spread about in the open.
Four small fires did occur, the largest taking
place in March, 1917. On that occasion piles
of ammunition were lying in close proximity

to a wharf where artillery supplies were being discharged. At the next berth were piles of nitrate. Close by great stacks of crated cotton caught fire. It was providential that the wind bore the flames and sparks away from the nitrate, the ammunition and the artillery supplies, otherwise an immense amount of devastation would have taken place.

The Port Commandant, realising the danger, lost no time in procuring three good motor fire engines and a number of tugboats equipped with powerful pumps.

The Stevens Commission had to face the fact that Vladivostok had seen 1,840,000 tons of cargo arrive in 1916. I checked over some of the railway figures in Vladivostok and tried to get an idea of how many sixteen-ton wagons actually left for the west each day. On one day in September, 1916, 103 cars left. Three days in October showed 166, 96 and 177, respectively. In November, one day saw 40 leave and another 108. Two checkings in December showed 90 and 71. An average day in January, 1917, saw but 31 depart, while three days in February gave the following figures, 51, 94, and 136. So they ran on. Two days in March showed 69 and 66. Two days in April, 51 and 70. Two in May, 81 and 139. Two in June, 118 and 103. Two in July 129 and 102; two in August, 49 and 38; two in September, 94 and 96.

Under the plans made by the Stevens Commission, three hundred wagons as a minimum were to leave Vladivostok daily and it was expected that the number would be increased to four hundred. The original plan was to supply many thousand wagons, thousands of locomotives and thousands of coal cars. Plans were made to erect these at Vladivostok, in numbers of hundreds per day. The scheme was an ambitious one and meant the arrival in Vladivostok of a million tons of cargo, including a half million tons of rails. This would necessitate the employment of three hundred steamers for six months, at the rate of fifty per month, allowing 16 to 19 days' time for discharge, and that very little else would come into Vladivostok for six months except railway material. The labour question presented all sorts of difficulties in this connection. The Chinese are the best available class of labour, and at first the Russians were not inclined to let the Chinese labour come in. This was gotten over somewhat, however, by the proposal of the Chinese to join the Russian labour union. I asked one of the American railway men, who was best qualified to judge, what he thought of the average Russian railway engineer.

"He is a good employé and a good workman and knows how to handle his engine," was the reply.

The Americans were somewhat amused at the system that obtained of one man to one engine. When the engineer slept, the engine slept. Thus, due to the fact that but one driver was allowed to handle one locomotive, the engine would only cover two thousand miles in the space of time in which it might be expected to travel three thousand. Examination of repair books and records showed that the percentages of "sick" engines were not high. This was evidence that the Russian railway engineer took good care of his machine.

When the American Railway Commission reached Petrograd, it sought to ascertain the theory upon which empties were sent back from Russia to Vladivostok, but no man could make much headway with the tangle into which things had gotten along this line. All Russian railways were short of rolling stock, and the Trans-Siberian Railway had to suffer in consequence. A committee handled the disposition of the empties and gave orders for their despatch to various centres and over various roads. A

Russian friend of mine spent all one night proving to me that this committee was actuated by pro-German sentiment, if in fact it was not paid by German gold. He could produce no little evidence of actions on the part of the committee which looked very much as though they were deliberately planned to hamper the efficient working of the railway. I could sympathise with his point of view, and whether or not the committee could be convicted of effort to help Germany, the Boche had the assistance, indirectly.

Stevens came to the conclusion that young American railway men as general superintendents, heads of the engineering departments and general managers, as well as chief despatchers and line superintendents would be invaluable to the Trans-Siberian Railway. The Russians seemed eager and anxious to learn, and were only waiting for the coming of some one who could teach them. In spite of the shortage of railway men which the coming of the war would make inevitable in America, some three hundred picked men were sent from the United States to Vladivostok in 1917. For various reasons they were diverted temporarily to Japan instead of commencing their work of reorganisation in Siberia.

The outbreak of the Revolution in 1917 and the formation of the Committee of Public Safety in Vladivostok had but little effect at first on the railway situation. A new Commissioner from Petrograd was started eastward to take over the administration of the railway and control the despatch of goods from Vladivostok. This Commissioner, Petrograd decreed, was to be assisted by a committee formed from the heads of local departments and such public bodies as the Committee of Public Safety and the Council of Soldiers' and Workmen's Deputies. Pending the arrival of this Commissioner, the Commandant of the Fortress was in charge of all shipping matters and his chief assistance came from the transport section of the Committee of Public Safety. This sub-committee was formed by the main body solely to prevent abuses on the railway. Some of the Soldiers' and Workmen's Deputies who could be found advising matters relating to shipping and transport knew nothing whatever of the work in hand, and had no knowledge of either railway or steamship lines. Their interference was sometimes annoying, but for the most part they were content with seeing that matters were conducted in accordance with their idea of fairness and right.

THE FANATIC ELEMENT

CHAPTER X

The Fanatic Element

As the months of 1917 rolled by it became evident that the more rabid element among the Russian politicians was gaining strength rather than losing in Vladivostok.

The average business man in the city would tell you, with a shrug of his shoulders or a gesture of despair, that the worst element among the people had gotten hold of the reins of government. In Vladivostok I came into contact with several men, whose judgment should have been sound, who had become hopeless regarding the situation. The chief difficulty in trying to get an accurate line on just how matters stood was the unreliability of report. Some Russian would tell me that the people in power politically were anxious to split up all the property in the town, immediately and without compensation to owners of land or buildings. Others denied that this was the case.

I became somewhat curious to know just what

183

was being advocated by the Russians in Vladivostok who were closest in touch with affairs and who were in the seat of government, if not the seat of power.

Great care had to be taken in ascertaining whether or not a Russian politician was a representative of the government at Petrograd or was one of the Vladivostok crowd. One of the first things I learned about the Russian element who were closest to the government was that they were men from entirely different classes. I knew one sober, thoughtful fellow, who had never been in the least an agitator, who had worked hard in America and come back to Russia with an honest desire to serve his fellow-men. Closely associated with him was one of the most visionary and erratic anarchists with whom I have ever met. These men disagreed on many points, but hung together on some fundamental theories, with which their minds were both full. It did not seem to worry the quiet, thoughtful chap that his friend was utterly mad on several very important subjects. He seemed oblivious of that. He would discuss with me his friend's ideas and condemn some of them frankly, but he seemed to think that on the whole they were each working together for a common end, though trying to achieve it by

different methods. He was not so much interested in the manner in which the goal which he
sought might be reached, as in the fact that he
and his friend were impelled by desire for the
establishment of the same ultimate conditions.

A socialist meeting in the Russian Far East
has an atmosphere all its own.

In a big empty factory building in Siberia,
silent machines grouped round as if in mute
protest at the interruption of their daily work,
Russian men and women gathered in the afternoon of a pleasant autumn day.

Admission to the meeting was easily gained.
Any one could come. Each member of the audience was supposed to contribute a piece of
silver at the door, but many drifted in without
paying any attention to the collection box.

I was an early arrival. I stood by the barrier, through a small gate in which the incom-
ing crowd had to pass, and watched the faces.

Men were there, and women, who were toil-
ers in that very factory. Others were work
people of other factories, not far distant, whose
machinery was idle, too. It was not a day for
work. It was a lazy day. The air was soft.
Even the sun shone lazily. I was lazy, and I
pride myself I am rarely lazy. Why, then,
should not the Russians have been lazy—so

many of whom are born lazy and never get over it?

They came in quietly enough. Some of the men were fine looking fellows. Some of the women were comely, but none of them handsome. They were a stolid lot. With the work people a few sailors drifted by, then a group of soldiers, and last a score of students.

I recognized one or two men who might be described as bourgeois. Trimming their sails to the wind, they were. But few of the bourgeois had either sufficient courage, sufficient common sense, or sufficient patriotism to try to guide the more socialistic elements in Siberia. If any class in Russia has failed utterly to grasp the slightest conception of its duty toward itself, its brethren, the State, or humanity, it is the bourgeois class in Russia. True, it has had a rough passage. But it cringed and ran. It did not stay and help—except in rare instances. It loved its wealth, such as it had, more than it loved Russia.

The Bolsheviki are bad enough, but I had rather be a Bolshevik than a bourgeois in Russia, if I was to condemn myself to the line of action that either class has taken.

Piles of metal lay about. Along one wall were rods of steel which should have been being

rapidly turned into bolts on the screw machines
not far away. I suppose I was the only person
present who thought that the socialists might
be better engaged in working the lathes and
drills than in listening to flowery orations on
the subject of the millennium. We seemed a long
way from the millennium that day in Siberia.

As I walked in with the crowd, and stood at
a point where I could be sure to hear the speaking, I became impatient with that audience, in-
dividually and collectively.

My impatience died, and I looked upon them,
as one should look upon them, as sober, misguided children.

They were so docile. They were so quiet and
orderly. They were in such deadly earnest.
They could not help being lazy. Most Russians are lazy. It is a lazy land. Very few
Russians have had any incentive in their lives
to be anything but lazy. It really hasn't mattered in Russia. The average Russian didn't
get on very much better, if he wasn't lazy. It's
all a matter of experience. If you start out
being lazy in this world, and nobody criticises,
and the necessaries of life come along naturally enough and pretty well the same as they come
to everybody else in the community, you drift.
A spark may be blown into a small blaze now

and again by the breeze of a passing inspira-
tion, but it dies down. Nobody cares. Nobody
notices. It's a hopeless business, being industrious all by yourself. All the more so—when it
isn't fashionable.

They were orderly, that audience. They were
patient. Russia stands for patience. It's a
monument of patience. A people could have a
worse attribute.

And so they filed in, there by the still machines, that seemed to me to be crying out to
be worked, and waited—with no disorder, with
no tumult, with no loud words. They were con-
siderate enough of one another coming in.
There was no pushing or shoving—no rudeness.
They were a bit bovine, perhaps, but very nice-
ly, very considerately so.

The soldiers were quiet. Typically Russian,
they were as patient as the work-folk. As I
stood there watching them my mind went back,
years into the past, to other days in Siberia.
I remembered the smooth-faced boy, the orderly of a drunken Russian colonel who had been
beaten to death by his master with a scabbard-
ed sabre, because he had failed to procure something for which he had been sent. That boy
died a violent death. He had lived a violent
life. Violence was an every-day experience to

him. The colonel, who was unpunished for his
crime, and was soon beating another orderly
at regular intervals, saw to it that any Russian
soldier with whom he came in constant contact,
had his share of violence.

But these Russian soldiers were not violent.
They were a bit restless, as if having no very
clearly defined plan, but they were not the sort
of men who would be violent, unless drunk.
There is no drink to be had in Siberia.

The big shop filled at length. Then there
was a commotion near the door and a lane opened. Down the lane came a trio, who were to
be the speakers of the afternoon.

Samelyoff, Parenogo and Commandantoff
were what their names sounded like to me.
Those were not the names, exactly, but as the
three speakers were none of them international
celebrities, it does not matter much what I call
them.

I instinctively liked Samelyoff. He was a big
chap, tall and strong. He had a fine chest and
well-set shoulders. His hair, brown, with red
lights, waved back picturesquely from his high
forehead. He was cleanshaven. His eyes were
brown, and large. His mouth was too small,
and weak, if one wished to be critical, but he
was a fine-looking young chap, for all that. He

was about thirty. From his dress I judged him a workman, but an acquaintance said no, he was a stranger who had drifted into Siberia since the revolution, and did no work.

Samelyoff was the first speaker. He talked fluently enough, but the combined efforts of two quite good interpreters could not discover much sense in what he said. He was clearly a disciple of Karl Marx. To him there was only one class against whom to rail—the bourgeois. It mattered not what country was that of their origin. If they were what he called bourgeois, that was sufficient. He was against them and theirs. Peace without annexations and without indemnities came in for much of his time. He was so thoroughly convinced that the German workingman was about to rise and shake off the yoke of the Kaiser and his class, that it almost seemed a shame to disabuse his mind. The German working man was given more confidence by that odd, likable young Russian, than any one could appreciate, at first. The German workers were not only to overthrow Junkerism in Germany, but were to place back in Russia's hands all which she had lost during the war, as well as to restore complete liberty to Poland. The German working man was the friend, apparently, to whom the Russian brother must look for succour.

No man who saw and heard Samelyoff and had met with no others of his type could have imagined him anything but a German agent. I had seen too many like him, however, to think that was necessarily true. Many a young Russian enthusiast who would not take a penny of German money, or willingly aid the Prussian regime in any way, has spread broadcast through Russia doctrines that might well have had their inception in the very headquarters of German propaganda. They served the Boche as well, did these misguided folk, as if they had been in German pay.

Parenogo was a little man. He had a head like a spaniel, with a mane of wavy black hair. Most of the harangue was taken up with a dissertation on the character of the Russian revolution. Parenogo argued that the co-operation of the middle classes must be excluded. The government must be purely by the people. A world social revolution, he was convinced, was inevitable, and we were standing on the threshold of it. Peace, he said, should be made by democracy and not by diplomats. Democracy must fight for general disarmament.

The crowd listened attentively, and there

were no dissenting voices raised. One hardly
needed to understand Parenogo's words to realise that he considered himself a man with a
message. He felt what he said and was convinced that no argument would hold against
him.

Commandantoff, the third speaker, was another firebrand against the bourgeois. He
wanted to sweep the bourgeois out of every position and declared that the Workmen's and
Soldiers' Council, a council composed of true
revolutionaries, must have all the power in their
hands. He began to speak of dividing up the
land. Every workman was to have shorter
hours. Every peasant was to have some ground
which he could call his own. The State was to
control all industry, and an equalisation of
wealth was to be assured.

Commandantoff was a big fellow, with a
breadth of shoulder and depth of chest, and his
words rolled forth sonorously, his promises
falling on eager ears. The audience took increased interest in what he was saying. There
was not one voice raised to question him or to
point out the impossibilities in some of his suggested schemes. He talked on and on, drawing
a more and more roseate picture of the Russia
that was to come. He, too, was convinced that

the rest of the nations would follow in the footsteps of revolutionary Russia. The workmen
of the world would wipe out national boundary
lines and become an internationalist group,
swaying the world toward social democracy
until the rich no longer existed as a class, and
there were no poor in any land.

When the meeting broke up, people were
quite enthusiastic. Their simplicity was so
marked and their gullibility so great that these
specious phrases of the socialistic orators took
away their breaths for the moment.

I tried to find out to what extent these doctrines had really been adopted by the audience,
and the result was more encouraging than I
had anticipated. The Siberians seemed inclined
to question some of the axioms which had been
laid down so dogmatically by the speakers. I
was in the home of a Russian acquaintance,
questioning him as to the extent to which such
revolutionary doctrines were imbibed on short
notice when Commandantoff called. I was introduced to him and listened to him with close
attention for some time. I told him frankly
that I was in favour of the prosecution of the
war against Germany and that I did not sympathise particularly with the Russion bourgeois, for the reason that they had lost heart

to an extent which made one disgusted with them.

"I have come to the conclusion," I told him, "that the better educated classes of the Russian people throughout the whole country love their own. skins and their property as much as they love Russia. When the unconscious and ignorant masses of the people, particularly the men without education among the army and the labouring classes began to answer the Bolshevik call and agitate for social revolution, the more conscious elements of the Russian people threw up the sponge too quickly. Once the agitation was started and the call for class war was sounded, the Russian intelligent and educated classes, entirely unprepared for a struggle and seemingly with no capacity or capability of putting up a fight, retired and sulked in the corner, accepting at once the theory that they were powerless to stop the riot. By doing this they gave a free hand to the uneducated, loafing and totally unconscious bulk of the population, who were guided by extreme anarchists and socialists and who were continually misled, although sometimes unconsciously, by German agents. The fact that the bourgeois element has been guilty of less strenuous effort to help than might have been expected from it, does not mean that there are not good people among that class. They are Russians. Why do you not willingly accept their co-operation and assistance in making over Russia into a new Republic? Has not a man of the bourgeois as much right to be called a Russian as a man of the working classes?"

The argument Commandantoff used in reply was no answer to my question. Either he was utterly shallow and had adopted a number of high-sounding phrases and arguments from the leaders of the Bolsheviki, or he was incapable of argumentative reasoning. He talked bitterly against the Allies, but I could not get him into a state of mind where cohesive statements on one side or the other would lead to a continuity of reasoning. He admitted that there was a good deal of German propaganda going on in Russia, but immediately swung to the argument that there was a great deal of Socialist propaganda going on in Germany. The poor fellow was undoubtedly of the opinion that Russian propaganda would win against Germany no matter how much German propaganda might be used in Russia. He asked me if I did not think the Allies were at fault for not having supported Russia by recognising the Bolshevik government.

"The decomposition of the victualling and

transport organisation in Russia became an excellent ally for German agitation," I replied, "and the fault of the Allies lay in the fact that they did not earlier pay sufficient attention to these two serious questions. On the other hand, every difficulty was put in the way of Allied effort to assist. The Allied missions which were sent to Russia lacked sympathy with the objects of the extremists who were exploiting the real power in Russia, and an impasse under such circumstances was inevitable. The Allies, however, could not make a certain section of the Russian army fight longer in this war. Nevertheless, a section, a considerable section, of the Russian army would fight against Prussian militarism. It is you and speakers like you who argue against the continuation of the war on any grounds who are forcing your country under the feet of Germany, and the first thing they will trample out of the prostrate body of Russia will be the fruits of the Russian revolution."

Some of the statements I made Commandantoff inquired into through my friend who was doing the interpreting for us. He thought a moment, and then said, "What you say seems sensible in some ways, but you fail to take into consideration the fact that the German work-

man and the Austrian workman have in their
hearts the same ideals which we have. Would
you like to know what I consider our new Russia should be? It should be a country where
there were no men who did not work produc-
tively for at least five hours every day, if not
six. The remainder of the day should be at
the entire disposal of the individual. The State
should control all industries so that no monopo-
lies would be possible. Great riches could not
be amassed and the State should see to it that
there was work for every one, so that there
would be no misery and poverty. The Imperial
Romanoff Government went into this war for
no such ideals. England and France are not
fighting for such a result to the war. England
and France are fighting for industrial and commercial interests or for a gain of territory."

I broke in here to try to prove to him that
England and France were fighting for something else, but Commandantoff was not anxious
to hear new theories on that head. The base on
which all his arguments were reared took into
account first the fact that he was the advocate
of something higher and better for Russia,
something more ideal and more honestly to be
sought than any object of any other country in

the war. To argue that the Allied nations were in any way right was tearing from under him some of the platform on which he stood. He could have no sympathy with that.

"If you can show me how continuing to fight Germany would change the mind of England and France as to the sort of government they should have, the way the workmen of their country should be treated, and the attitude their people should take against the rights of property," he said, "I would be interested to hear it."

His words were utterly untrue. He was not in the least interested to hear anything which combatted his arguments. There was only one view for him, and that was the one that had been given him in Petrograd. Curiously enough, I think he was conscientiously of the belief that he was right. He simply had a total incapacity for argument or for reason.

That is the class of man that in many instances one finds in Russia and the Russian Far East, and a little well directed educational work to counteract the influence of this type would wipe away much of the poison from the minds of the people. A campaign of education is a positive necessity if the Russians throughout

their whole empire are to gain any more intelligent ideas than those which are being fed to
them by such men as those to whom I listened
that afternoon in the empty factory building.

GERMAN PROPAGANDA

CHAPTER XI

German Propaganda

No man who has not come into touch with it can appreciate the depth and subtlety of German propaganda. I have seen so much of it in different parts of the world since 1914 that I am beginning to recognise the earmarks once in a while, before I can trace the actual source of operation.

When walking along a street in a town in Siberia, one might come into frequent contact with soldiers and sailors and hold short conversations on different topics. Neither soldiers nor sailors had much to do. Strolling along one morning in Vladivostok, a British officer whom I knew met a fine, clean-looking young Russian sailor. As the boy passed the officer, he paused a moment and addressed him in Russian. Fortunately my friend could speak Russian well. He smilingly returned the salutation of the young bluejacket. We always smile in Russia; it never fails to bring an answering smile. The Russian boy was clear-eyed, open-faced, and his smile was good to see.

"Would you mind if I asked you a question?" he asked my friend the Major.

"Certainly not," was the reply. "You are quite at liberty to ask anything that you like."

"We are much interested in your uniform," said the young Russian. "We have seen it several times now, and we have had one or two discussions as to just what uniform it is. If you do not mind my asking you, I should like to know if it is the uniform of a Turkish general or of an American lieutenant."

"How in the world did you come to the conclusion that it might be one or the other?"

"I did not. One of the boys said he thought it looked like the uniform of a Turkish general. He has been in Constantinople, and he thought he knew. Another of my comrades said he was sure it was an American uniform and thought it might be that of a lieutenant."

The Major laughed heartily. "My uniform is that of a regiment known as the Black Watch. It is a British uniform."

"Really! How interesting. The boys will be pleased to know that."

The sailor was about to pass on down the street, when my friend stopped him and asked,

"How could you think that my uniform was that of a Turkish officer when you know that your country is at war with Turkey? If I were the Turkish general I could not be here in Vladivostok."

"Ah," replied the sailor, "that would have been so a few days ago. But now that the revolution in Turkey has come and we are no longer at war with Turkey, there is no reason that you could not be here, even were you a Turkish general, is there?"

"But no Turkish revolution has taken place, my boy," said the Major.

"Have you not heard the news?" came from the sailor. "Do you not know that the people in Turkey have overthrown their rulers as we did in Russia? Do you not know that Turkey, too, is governed by Committees of Soldiers' and Workmen's Deputies?"

"I do not know that," said the Major, with a smile. "In fact, I know that such is not the case, unfortunately. No; Russia is still at war with Turkey. There is no peace for the South of Russia yet, and no peace in immediate prospect, unless it would be one that would be worse than war."

The sailor's eyes brightened and he smiled back, delighted to find some one to whom

he could impart newly gathered information.
"Then my news is later than yours," he said.
"Come with me to the barracks and I will show
you. I have proof that what I say is true."

The Major walked down with him, and there
in the barracks the boy produced a printed
sheet in Russian, giving all the details of the
Turkish revolution—telling all the story in a
clever, detailed way, ably compiled to catch the
mind and the imagination of just such bright
young Russian boys. No need to ask where that
sheet originated. No need to ask the source of
that news. That poison came straight from
Germany.

Fortunate it was that the Major had that casual conversation on the pavement that morning,
for he was able to hammer home some plain
truths, not only about that highly imaginative
account of the Turkish revolution, but about
the methods of the men who had manufactured
the information for Russian consumption.

The Austrian and German prisoners were
sometimes visited by neutral officials. Before
America's entrance into the war a citizen of the
United States had this duty to perform. When
I was in Siberia I met a Swedish gentleman of
rank, whose ostensible labours in the Russian
Far East were to report, as an unbiassed ob-

server, on the manner in which the Russians were treating the prisoners from the armies of the Central Powers.

On more than one occasion the Swedish gentleman indulged in close conversation with some Russian. Usually it was an employé of the government or a soldier in the army, but the Swedish gentleman was nothing if not catholic in the selection of his acquaintances.

"You poor fellows," was the gist of one conversation which was overheard. "You splendid Russians. Is it not a pity that after you have fought so hard and so well for such a long time, and after you have suffered so terribly and had such awful casualties, that you should find yourselves where you are now? What a shame that after the sacrifices you have made in this war for the Allies, that they should have deserted you now, just as you have thrown off the yoke of your old government and are trying so hard and so splendidly to formulate your new Republic. My heart goes out to you. I feel that it is terribly unjust that the Allies should refuse to recognise your new government. How ungrateful of the Allies, after all that you have done for them in the way of bloodshed and loss, that they should turn from you now and fail to give you their sympathy or

support. You poor fellows. Apparently the
only friend you have left is Germany—at least,
if Germany is not a friend, she seems inclined
to treat you fairly and to make a peace which
will prevent your going on with the paying of
so heavy a price in the interests of those Allies
of yours. It is they who gain and you who lose.
You may indeed count yourselves fortunate that
Germany is not so heartless."

The Swedish gentleman was spreading that
sort of stuff wherever he went.

"Made in Germany?" Unquestionably.

There were people around Siberia who were
talking against the Allies, who were not paid
by German gold nor subsidised by German influence. I met such a one in a conference I was
holding with some of the newspaper editors in a
city in Siberia. One of the most important pub-
lications in that locality was what attempted to
be the daily organ of the Soldiers' and Workmen's Deputies. It was intended to be a "daily"
right enough, but it was very spasmodic. It
was run by a committee. The editor was a soft-
voiced, simple, quiet Russian, who, fortunately
for me, knew that my views toward labour were
decidedly liberal. In fact, he introduced me
to the rest as a socialist, although he explained
that I was about twenty-five years behind the

times. I discovered that he had been a reporter on a labour paper in Brisbane, Australia, and had there reported an address of mine in which I put forward certain views with which the labourites were at that time in sympathy. That effort of mine in Australia aimed to show that there were some of us outside the Socialist group who held fairly broad-minded ideas about the progress of humanity, proved to have been bread cast upon the waters.

I visited the editorial rooms of this Soldiers' and Workmen's paper in Siberia with no little anticipation. The leading minds that had to do with the paper were present, as well as one or two other editors of similar papers. One of these was the editor of a paper called the *Red Banner,* which promulgated the views of the Maximalist extremists.

My friend from Australia interpreted for me, as he did many times afterwards, proving most helpful and offering his services cheerfully and willingly. He was a nice boy.

On this particular occasion there were several present who could speak some English. After some little time, when I had become fairly started on the subject of the war and we were getting pretty close together on the question of how more and better war news could be placed before them, a young fellow came in, sat down and rather unceremoniously joined the conversation. He was a pale, æsthetic looking young man, a Jew, with straight black hair and very black eyes under heavy eyebrows. I saw the stamp of the fanatic on him at once. I was really interested in hearing the views of the Russian newspaper men, and they were thoroughly interested in what I was telling them in return. For this reason I did not warmly welcome the intervention of the black-haired one. However, I smiled. Smiles were of no use to him. He was not of the smiling kind. His heart was bitter.

"Do you criticise the conditions that you find here?" he asked.

"Yes," I replied, "some of them."

"Before you do that you had better go home to America and look into your own conditions," he said venomously.

I smiled. "I have looked into the conditions in my own country lots of times," I said. "Moreover, I have looked into the conditions of a good many countries besides my own."

"After what America has done to Russia you should be ashamed to come here," he said, his black eyes darting fire as he spoke.

I smiled again. It was a little forced that time.

"America has certainly done Russia no harm," I replied.

"There has been a conspiracy between America and Japan to put down the price of the ruble," he said, striking his fist on the arm of his chair.

That remark delivered him into my hands for the moment. I had no difficulty in winning that argument. It required no eloquence or gift of debate to prove that America had done more than any other nation in the world to raise the price of the ruble.

But this made the black-haired one more bitter. As I turned to the question which we had been discussing before his arrival and spoke of the necessity that the Russian labouring man should give us of his best in Siberia, the fanatic thrust himself forward again.

"The Russian workingman," he said, "is further advanced than the American workingman. He knows what he wants and he is going to get it."

I ventured the suggestion that the American workingman was very well off comparatively. This caused a storm. For some minutes I had to listen to a denunciation of America which failed to amuse me,—and for once I stopped smiling. The fanatic held the floor with a tirade against American plutocracy, and what he said about the conditions under which American labour had to work sounded to me most exaggerated.

"In my youth I worked at manual labour," I told him. "Later I have been a director of more than one company which employed thousands of workers in different parts of the world. You are drawing a picture of American labour conditions which is untrue and unfair."

He declared that he was not. He declared that he had worked in America and knew what he was talking about. Spurred on by my contradiction, his abuse of America got beyond all bounds. I smelt the air of battle for a minute and, waiting until he was out of breath, took the opportunity to gain the floor and told him what I thought of him and his theories.

"You are the sort of Russian," I said, "who is working more harm than good in this country. You may not intend to do so. You are of the type that is always denouncing somebody or something. Condemnation is your forte."

I waited until my editor friend had translated my few sentences and then continued, "Your work in the world will always be destructive and never constructive. You love driving a wedge where you can and ripping things asunder. I'll guarantee that when you came to Siberia you started at once to try to make trouble between whatever factions you could find sufficiently patient to listen to you. You are an obstructionist and a partitionist. If I was a Russian the first thing I would do would be to banish some of your kind. This is the day for every Russian to join hands.''

That started one of the hottest arguments which I heard in Russia or Siberia. Several people took a hand in it. I learned afterwards that the black-haired one was, luckily for my analysis of his character, a firebrand of the worst type who had caused some trouble in Siberia. He had been sent out by the Provisional Government in connection with some official work and was truly the sort of man who had a good word for no one. He was bitterness personified.

I do not know how far we succeeded, he or I, in transmitting our views to those who were listening to us. One or two of the journalists told me afterward that the fanatic had overreached himself and that my attack on him and his class and type had stung all the more, because it was true and deserved. I asked one of the journalists why this representative from Petrograd was so bitter against America.

"What did America ever do to him?" I asked.

"I will tell you," was the reply. "That boy has been a revolutionary from childhood. He was born one. His father used to take him to underground meetings when he was a mere baby. The father and the child with him were under suspicion for some years and finally, when evidence against the father was procured and he was ordered deported to Siberia, not many years passed before the boy was sent to the mines as well. His revolutionary tendencies grew fast under restraint. He was always in trouble with the authorities. For six long years of his early manhood he wore ball and chain on wrist and ankle. Finally he escaped and obtained permission to accompany a compatriot who was going to America. He landed in the United States almost penniless, found his way to the Atlantic seaboard, and obtained employment in the Bethlehem mines.

"From what he has told me of the conditions under which he worked, they may be open to improvement. He could not stand the strain. Obtaining transportation by chance, he left the north and next landed in New Orleans."

"What a place for a white labouring man, who spoke little English, to find a job," I commented.

"So I should gather from what he has told me," my friend continued. "He did not stay in New Orleans long but drifted out to Texas. He knew little of how to make a living, and succeeded at it but poorly. I suppose he tried to disseminate some of his extreme Socialist ideas and that they met with an unpleasant reception in Texas. He says frankly sometimes that he was more than once knocked about."

I could see that thin-faced, black-haired young Russian, all nerves and fire, being roughly handled by some one who had considered physical violence the best reply to some of his arguments. I could see him snarl, too, when he was kicked.

"He disliked America, and when the Russian revolution came and he was given an opportunity to come back to Russia, he was glad to shake the dust of America from his feet. He has talked to me about your country more than once. He would not like to go there again. Is it natural that he should dislike America?"

I suppose so. I suppose he saw no right hand of fellowship reached toward him. Perhaps it was natural that he should dislike America.

There may be things in America that some of us would dislike if we would get into touch with them. I wonder.

I met that Russian afterwards, and talked further to him. I think he disliked me less on the occasion of our second encounter. No words of mine, however, could convince him that he was wrong about America; or that the conditions under which the American labouring man worked were better than he thought them. While I did not sympathise greatly with him from some standpoints, I could be sorry for him. After all, he was the victim of a system— of environments over which he certainly had but little control.

BACK TO JAPAN—AND HOME TO THE U. S. A.

CHAPTER XII

BACK TO JAPAN—AND HOME TO THE U. S. A.

IN passing through from Siberia, I found official Japan was ready and willing to send an army into the Russian Far East to guard the accumulated stores in Vladivostok and to take possession of the Trans-Siberian Railway. It would be futile for Japan to land troops in Vladivostok, without taking over the line as far to the eastward as Irkutsk. I heard many and varied stories of not unfriendly Russian action toward German and Austrian prisoners, but so far as Siberia is concerned, enemy prisoners had not been released at that time to any appreciable extent, and there was no menace at that moment from this source.

In Japan, one cannot but come into contact with the loud-voiced element which talks wildly of the amount of good to the Allied cause which Japan's actions thus far have accomplished. In newspaper offices, in business houses, in Japanese homes, in the universities and schools and in Governmental Departments, one continually finds Japanese who overestimate the value of Japan's services to the Allies. The taking of Kiao-chow, the convoying of the Australian troops, the occupation of some of Germany's islands in the Pacific and the work of Japan's fleet would be given more prominence and praise by the average traveller in Japan if the Japanese did not themselves so continually lay weight and stress upon these things.

The man in the street in Japan held such a diversity of views on all subjects connected with the war, that one had to make a veritable symposium of expressions of opinion to come to any definite conclusion as to the sympathy of the public or its lack of sympathy with the proposal to despatch an armed Japanese expedition to Siberia or Russia in support of the Allies.

Japan must be understood and the Japanese form of government must be understood before one can grasp the exact values of Japanese public opinion.

Terauchi and his Cabinet and their expressions are a much better guide to what may be expected of Japan than several dozen conversations with men who hold no particular place in affairs Japanese.

Count Terauchi told me plainly how he felt on the subject. He pledged Japan, so long as he is Premier, to do all in her power to help.

Count Terauchi told me very plainly that personally he had always been sorry that circumstances did not permit of Japan's armies taking the field against Germany. Terauchi is a military man and a real soldier. He knows, as many leading minds in Japan know, the vast difference between building up a military force on a militaristic basis in the way Germany did, and the maintenance of a strong army with a constant eye on adequate military preparation. Just as Japan must have the support of some allied naval power, so she must have some *quid pro quo* to offer as a basis for such alliance. Japan, armed and ready to preserve the peace of the Far East, may be just as much an asset to such a peace as she might be a menace to it. One rarely finds a middle view on this subject in the Far East. Japan and the Japanese talk so much about preserving the peace of the Far East that any one who is anti-Japanese sneers at the very expression. Nevertheless, the maintenance of no little military strength on the part of Japan might prove a very active factor in preventing the breaking out of trouble here and there, as it certainly has done, to some extent, in Siberia.

Terauchi is the strong man of the Orient. I like him and admire him. He is autocratic, but a fighter. The Island Empire could have no better hand on the reins than his when the day comes for her soldiers to move in their tens of thousands along the paths that lead to blood and fire. Terauchi has kept his troth with the Allies, too. I have no authority from him to say so, but I am perfectly certain he brought Japan as far as he could toward giving the Allies the shipping assistance they asked. But Terauchi cannot do miracles. The big shipping concerns are the money power in Japan, and Japan is no democracy. The influence and authority of big business in Japan is great. To realise how great try to find out, in big national matters in Japan, where the Mitsui Bussan Kaisha begins and where the government ends. Study the Mitsukoshi Company. Yes, big business is big business, and sometimes bad big business, in Japan. That is some of the materialism Japan has absorbed from the West.

Count Terauchi will be Premier of Japan, so far as human forecast can be made, until the end of the war. If Viscount Kato and the opposition of which he is the head were to prove

capable of ousting Terauchi from the **Premier-**
ship, they would have done so long before this.
They were able, owing to the constitution of
the Diet and the arbitrary nature of Terauchi's
appointment as Premier, to make him go to the
country in 1917. When he was returned to
power in the general election in the spring of
1917, he could indeed settle himself confidently
in his seat. The press of Japan has been against
him with few exceptions since the day he took
office. He has played the game with the Allies
and has been genuinely anxious, not only personally, but as the head of his government, to
do what lay in his power to get Japan more
whole-heartedly into the war.

I sought in Siberia some evidences, however
slight, that Japan had been doing otherwise
than playing the game in the Russian Far East,
in spite of the existence of conditions that con-
stituted in themselves some temptation. None
could I find.

On my last afternoon in Tokyo I spent two
very delightful hours with Viscount Motono,
Japan's able Foreign Minister. Matters had
not yet come to a head in Russia, but looked
very bad. Viscount Motono knows Russia well.
He is profoundly sympathetic with the Russians.

He probably realises more fully than most
of his countrymen would do, the extent to which
sending Japanese troops to Siberia would of-
fend Russian susceptibilities. At the same time,
he knows the disintegration and chaos that exist in Russia.

The policy that Japan must pursue, the policy
that Count Terauchi and Viscount Motono and
Japanese statesmen of that class are well aware
must be Japan's policy if she is to take high
place among the nations of the world, is open
and above-board from beginning to end.

Nothing would hurt Japan's position among
the nations of the West more than a move toward aggrandisement of territory in the Russian Far East. Japan knows that—or at least
those at the head of her affairs know it. In
spite of the fact that Japan is not a democracy
and that none of her statesmen who are in office to-day are democratic, in spite of her record in China, Japan will be most punctilious in
any action she may take in Siberia. Her troops
there will be very carefully watched from Tokyo
and no opportunity be given for just criticism
of their deportment or lack of discipline. Japan
may be trusted to do what she agrees to do.

Japan will play the game. Never mind what
ideas many Japanese have held before. Never

mind what ideas some of them hold now. Japan will play the game in Siberia beyond question. To do so will be the strongest move she can make toward the strengthening of her national security. The big men in Japan know this, and her biggest men control her policies and politics to-day.

Furthermore, it is Japan's best opportunity for increasing the scope of her industrial development in a way that other nations will find difficulty in describing as illegitimate or objectionable.

Last, but not least, it will afford Japan an opportunity for allaying some of the suspicions in which she is held. It will allow her to pursue her policy of trying to make Japan and the Japanese popular and gain her economic ends through peaceful persuasion and penetration, rather than the sort of force that is "made in Germany."

The need for recognition by the Allied governments, and by America, that no matter what happens in Russia Siberia can be saved, is imperative. Rumours that some organisation was to be effected among the German and Austrian prisoners in Siberia have taken such form as a semi-official statement to the effect that a Prussian General had been started from Germany to organise an army in Siberia from the prison camps. The number of Russian troops in Siberia must have reached, at the beginning of 1918, somewhere near 350,000. In spite of the dissemination of Bolshevik doctrines among them, a campaign of education would bring out a great deal of real sound patriotism from the soldier element. It would not be difficult to reorganise a section of the Russian army in Siberia.

One must remember that these men have been soaked and steeped in German propaganda. Ideas have been promulgated among them which would seem absurd to us, but which seem perfectly reasonable to them. The result is that on simple enough questions their perspective is all wrong. The Russian soldier in Siberia is not a coward, and if you can show him something to fight for there is plenty of fight left in him.

The taking over of Vladivostok and the Trans-Siberian Railway, at least so far west as Irkutsk, by the Japanese army, would preserve Siberia from German encroachment. If the question is handled rightly, a simultaneous reorganisation of the Russian army in Siberia might be carried into effect. It would assist **great**ly the effort to get the Russians into a frame of mind where they looked with less hostility on armed assistance from the Japanese. If they saw that the Japanese were not endeavouring to stifle some effort on the part of the Russians to assist in the protection of their own country, it would create a very different atmosphere.

Too much must not be looked for from the Japanese military group, by which I mean the army officers who would be in actual occupation of such territory as might be occupied by soldiers of Japan, for the reason that they are not distinguished by their tact. The Japanese army officer is not a very polite person when he is addressing some one who is to him obviously an inferior—this in spite of the fact that he is extremely polite to an equal. The current manner of a Japanese officer in carrying out instructions must be described as somewhat high-handed.

On the other hand, Count Terauchi knows his army and would undoubtedly take ample precautions to see that not only officers of high rank who might come into touch with the Russians in Siberia would handle the situation diplomatically, but that the rank and file of the Japanese army would cause just as little inconvenience and friction as possible. Where

there is this determination there is no need to
anticipate trouble. The effect that the entrance
of Japan into actual field operations would have
on the German people would probably be negligible. It would seem to the Germans impossible that a nation so far from its base as Japan
would be when operating west of Irkutsk would
be likely to prove a serious menace to German
military or political operations in European
Russia. The material for the entire change of
the efficiency of the Trans-Siberian Railway is,
however, available, and the Trans-Siberian line
under American supervision or under Japanese, for that matter, would prove a very different means of communication than formerly.
Once let the Japanese army take hold in the
Russian Far East, and it would at least prove
an effective menace to Germany and a nucleus
of a sort, if the matter is handled wisely, for
the reorganisation of some portions of the Russian army. After all, the Russians are simple-
minded folk. They are good natured and kind-
ly. They have been engineered into a dislike
and hatred for the Japanese, so far as the Siberians are concerned, which the Russian of
the West feels in much less degree.

There is great opportunity for an educational
campaign which would primarily let Japan save

from the Germans that much of Russia which she can effectively and practically reach, leaving the extent of her operations to the future and to the development of what part of the work she first embarks upon.

Once given a rallying point and a line of secure defence, recruiting for a new Russian army, an army with new heart, new life and new soul in its individual units, would be a less difficult task than might be anticipated.

I know men who could go to-morrow to regiments in Siberia, whose record has been one of some unrest, and gather around them sixty per cent, if not a greater proportion of the soldiers, who would follow them gladly to fight against Germany and German domination.

The sort of men who are needed in Russia from the English-speaking world are men who have sympathy with the Russians and confidence that in the end Russia will win through and escape disintegration as a nation.

Hope is a big factor toward effort. Imagine the position of some young Slav in the Russian army, who feels he could gather around him a number of his fellows who would continue to fight against Germany if they had a chance. Think of the amount of heart and hope that is taken out of such a man by hearing and reading repeatedly that the military representatives of the Allies have stated that there was no more fight left in the Russians. What the Allies say does not matter so much if it is said at home, for the reason that German propaganda sees to it that the spokesmen of the Allies are so utterly misrepresented in Russia. What the representatives of the Allies who are on the ground say is a very different matter. The men that could talk to the Russian soldiers and talk effectively are men who have been in uniform and fought on their own fronts,—and perhaps been wounded there.

I had good evidence of this in Vladivostok. A Y. M. C. A. representative there wore a khaki uniform and very unwisely obtained permission to wear with it insignia of rank as an officer. He came to one of the officers among the Allied representatives in Vladivostok and said, "You know the men of a certain artillery regiment with whom I would like to get in touch. Would you put me in the way of doing so?"

The officer saw the committee of this regiment and was surprised to hear them say, "We do not want that man to come to us and our men do not want him. He wears an officer's uniform, but he is not in the American army, is he? Why should he wear the uniform of an officer when he never has done and never intends to do any fighting? We do not want that kind of man here.''

The officer explained the situation to the Y. M. C. A. representative, whose action had been born of a mistaken idea as to the importance he would assume in the community if he wore the insignia of the rank that he had adopted. His idea was that it would impress the Russian soldier. It did impress him, but it impressed him the wrong way.

Avoidance of such little mistakes as this will make all the difference in handling the situation in Siberia. There is much good in the country and in the people. There is better opportunity, comparatively, to save the situation in Siberia than in Russia. America cannot wash her hands of her responsibilities toward any part of Russia. Help can come more easily from us than from any one else, and if the help is put forward in the right way, American help will be more welcome in the Russian Far East than help that can possibly come from any other source.

If Russia cannot save Siberia from the Hun and Japan can do so, Japan had best take on the job.

Japan stands to gain much, from the day her

columns march forth to war for the Allied cause. Much that she will gain may be material. Some of it may be moral and spiritual.

One thing is sure. Her national security will be strengthened in direct ratio to the numbers of her brave little men who may leave their lives in the Pri-Amur, should blood be shed there, or further off to the westward, where the camps of Armageddon may yet, one day, echo to the tramp of the legions from the Land of the Rising Sun.

But of greater importance than the national security of Japan is the barrier in the path of German plans and ambitions that will be thrown in her way by the full participation of Japan in the war.

That participation will bring the day of Peace nearer—the day of a Peace of the right sort— a Peace born of an unequivocal defeat of Germany on the field of battle.

No other Peace can be other than a victory in disguise for Germany. No other Peace can be a Peace for long.

THE END